Neither
BLACK nor WHITE
Just
DIFFERENT

Neither Black nor White

nor White

Just Different

Heather E Komagum

XULON PRESS

Xulon Press
2301 Lucien Way #415
Maitland, FL 32751
407.339.4217
www.xulonpress.com

Song: Here I am
Words by Chris Bowater
Copyright 1981 Sovereign Lifestyle Music Ltd
Used by permission

Sovereignmusic@aol.com

Printed in the United States of America.

ISBN-13: 978-1-54565-134-6

Through a powerful story of a young girl called to serve God in an amazing adventure in Africa, the author shares her wild and wonderful experiences that explore the victories, difficulties, and beautiful yet challenging diversity of life in Uganda. From her marriage to an African pastor to her personal spiritual growth, the author's story is a testament to the hand of God at work all over the world.

ACKNOWLEDGEMENTS

Thank you to everyone who has been a part of my journey in life – family, friends, colleagues on three continents. Each of you has impacted my life in one way or another, whether you realise it or not.

Thank you to the friends in my early days in Uganda, who prayed for me and helped me to stick in and see things through, even when it was hard.

Thank you to my MAF colleagues who were my family when I got married to Chris in Kampala. Special thanks to Vi Snaith, my matron.

Thank you to a lady I met at Colour Conference, Sydney, Australia many years ago, who provoked me to write a book to tell the world how a cross cultural marriage CAN work. That was the start of it all...

Thank you for those who took their precious time to read the manuscript and helped me improve on it.

Thank you finally to Cory for the beautiful photographs and to Brenda for bringing out the best in us as Cory snapped away to get the "perfect shot".

May the Lord richly bless each and every one of you as only He can.

Photographs by Cory McClay
Based in Surrey BC, Canada
Contact at corymcclay@hotmail.com

DEDICATION

This book is dedicated to my wonderful husband. He loved me, saw potential in me, believed in me, and encouraged me to grow in gifting and abilities that I wasn't even aware of. We are enjoying an amazing journey through life together... To my wonderful children, now teenagers, who are helping me to grow and mature as they stretch me.

To Stuart and Katharine, my special brother and sister-in-law, who braved coming to Africa to visit us on several occasions, making us feel so appreciated and valued. Thank you for the fun, laughter and love.

To Chris and Ros Woodman, whom God used to encourage me and propel me on my journey from Scotland to Uganda. Thank you for your continued belief in us.

To the pastors who have taught me the Word of God and have had spiritual input in my life:

Rev Bill Freel, Inverness Baptist Church

Elders of Nairn Baptist Church

Rev Larry Pumpelly and Rev John Ekudu, Kampala Baptist Church

Rev Gary Skinner, Kampala Pentecostal Church, now Watoto Church

Rev Sam Owusu, Calvary Worship Centre, Surrey BC

To all our praying friends, who continually remember us before our Heavenly Father. May the Lord reward you for your time spent and your tears shed on our behalf.

Above all, I acknowledge and thank my Lord and Saviour Jesus Christ. Without Him, there wouldn't have been a story at all.

ENDORSEMENTS

Heather & Chris have shared how a cross-cultural marriage can work in the best sense of the word, particularly when based upon a close relationship with God. Their cultural differences are shared in a very readable and honest way that not only provides practical help for those already in, or contemplating, a cross-cultural marriage, but also gives valuable guidelines for any marriage. They clearly demonstrate that it is possible to overcome all sorts of potential pitfalls with an open and honest approach. They confront potential problems all the way through their relationship, with a genuine sense of humility and humour that honours their deep commitment to serving Christ, in a world that has devalued commitment of any kind, especially in marriage.

Max Gove
Former MAF pilot, serving in various leadership roles from 1972 – 2015, and as CEO from 1991-1995

Personal stories allow us to see the beauty of God's grace lived out in contexts and places different from our own. Heather has opened the windows of her life lived with Chris, her soulmate and partner, and she allows us to see how they have crossed bridges that reduce cultural differences. Chris and Heather love and live the truth of the gospel and they show that Jesus is the one who breaks down walls of division. Her descriptions of Africa's rich culture, hospitality, communities and worship remind me of my own 35 years lived on a continent that is special, that I still call home. This story will be helpful to anyone who wishes to dig deep into cultural diversity.

Rev. D. Murray Cornelius, BScHons, MCS (Regent College)
Executive Director for International Missions
The Pentecostal Assemblies of Canada

Though Heather and Chris come from different hemispheres, they have bridged their cultural divide. Indeed, they validate my view that skin colour is just a matter of environmental convenience.

Bishop Henry Luke Orombi
Rtd Archbishop of Church of Uganda 2004 - 2012

TABLE OF CONTENTS

ACKNOWLEDGEMENTS vii
DEDICATION ix
ENDORSEMENTS xi
FOREWORD xv
INTRODUCTION xvii

1. My Background and Call 1
2. First Experience in Africa 11
3. Life in Uganda 19
4. Joy Grindey, the Unsung Missionary Heroine 23
5. The KPC Introduction. 29
6. Chris's Family Background 33
7. Experiencing the Ugandan Culture 41
8. The Cross-Cultural Dating Experience 45
9. The MAF Story Continued. 53
10. The Cross-Cultural Wedding Experience 57
11. The Cross-Cultural Honeymoon Experience 61
12. The Cross-Cultural Extended Family Experience 65
13. The Cross-Cultural Clashes 69
14. The Miraculous Provision 73
15. Cross-Cultural Concepts 77
16. Cross Cultural Adoption 83
17. Encountering Corruption 89
18. Cross-Cultural Paradigms 97
19. Cross-Cultural Compliments. 105

CONCLUSION 111
AFTERWORD. 113

FOREWORD

Heather and I have known each other since the early '90s. She worked with Mission Aviation Fellowship (MAF), whose little planes saved us so much time as we were living in the northern part of Uganda. I was a busy young archdeacon, serving as the *then* bishop's immediate administrative and pastoral assistant. On his retiral, I was subsequently appointed bishop, and later archbishop, by God's grace.

Whilst serving in the MAF office, I came to admire Heather's love for her work. She excelled in her tasks and had a love of helping others. With Heather around, things moved smoothly, and her colleague, Ruth, stood by her as another pair of hands to ensure all was in order.

Heather was created for Uganda right from the beginning. Reading her accounts about life in Uganda in those early days gives the reader a great insight into her life serving the Lord. She is balanced in sharing both her experiences and the things God taught her while living in Uganda. She braved the various aspects of life in the city of Kampala and is very observant about rural life, which makes her book very informative to read.

I have found out through her testimonies that God, who gave her Chris as a husband, brought her to Uganda to find out that He had answered her quest beautifully. Chris is a true believer, has a gentle character and is an effective pastor, whom she has wonderfully complemented.

The cross-cultural experiences she has tried to paint in this book are invaluable reading to couples who are walking that road, and the book would be good preparation for those who are planning to embark on a similar journey. In the biblical story of Ruth, at 1:16 it says: 'But Ruth replied, "Don't urge me to leave you or to turn back from you. Where you go I will go, and where you stay I will stay. Your people will be my people and your God my God"'.

That is also true for Heather. These are the words that kept ringing in my ears as I read her book – she followed God until she came to a place of great blessings. Indeed, Heather is a blessing to many people in Uganda, simply by being herself.

Couples should read her brief thoughts at the conclusion of the book because they spring from years of marital experience with Chris.

May I encourage you to read this little book because when I took it up, I couldn't stop until I finished it! Both Chris and Heather are great friends in the Lord Jesus, and I love them.

Bishop Henry Luke Orombi
Rtd Archbishop of Church of Uganda 2004 - 2012

INTRODUCTION

I f anyone had told me ten years ago that I would be living in the bush in the middle of Africa, sleeping on a dirt floor in a mud hut with no roof and watching the stars, I'd have said they were crazy! Ten weeks after marrying my Ugandan husband, Chris, that's exactly what we were doing. We had travelled upcountry, just after Christmas, to visit Chris's parents in rural north-central Uganda. We had sent money in advance of our arrival to pay for our house to be built. You see, once a young man reaches puberty, he is considered an adult. He is then supposed to build a house for himself, within or close to the circle of his family's several houses. He is too big now to sleep with the children, and he is expected to have his own house to take his future wife to.

Since Chris had moved to Kampala to stay with his older sister in 1973, he had not had the opportunity to build his own house. Our marriage precipitated the need for us to have our own place, and so we expected to find our new house ready for us. Well, *house* was a grand term. In reality, it was a circular mud hut, or *ot-lum* as it is called in Luo. By the time we got there, the building team hadn't quite completed our home—to say the least! The women had managed to erect the walls with still-damp mud blocks, but the door and window were just gaping, unfinished holes. The wooden frame that the men had made from tree branches for the roof was in place on top of the walls. But there hadn't been enough daylight hours to position and tie the sheaves of dried grass on the frame, which would cover the roof and make it wind- and watertight.

Fortunately for us, it was the dry season, and so we knew it would not rain in on us. The doorway was closed by means of a rusty old corrugated iron sheet placed across the doorway gap. It was held in place from the inside by an old armchair. This makeshift door would at least stop the flock of curious goats from entering in the morning and would give us some privacy. The window space had a mud brick sitting in it to close it in— almost. We didn't have any furniture, either. I think we'd forgotten to organise that. But at least we had a mattress to sleep on, which we placed on a mat made of dry papyrus reeds right on the dirt floor. I was comforted by the fact that the very-necessary mosquito net, when tucked in around and underneath the mattress, would keep out any unwanted creepy crawlies or snakes. With our crisp, clean sheets, cosy blanket and plumped up pillows, the bed looked really inviting come bedtime, and was, in fact, quite comfortable!

As we lay side by side, just talking over the day, that's when I made the unforgettable comment about our rather unusual— to say the least—circumstances.

Indeed, ten years earlier, Africa had been just a name—a place where there were wars, drought and famine. Little did I know then how my life would change and the direction it would take. So, how did it happen?

CHAPTER 1

My Background and Call

I grew up in a middle-class home in England and went to a girl's school where the students were mostly polite, well-behaved and eager to learn. Life was fun, and I especially loved my school days, even the dinners, would you believe! School was a wonderful experience, and I looked forward to it every day. When I started school at the tender age of four and a half, my mum tearfully led me up the school path. I was the last of her children to go to school, the end of an era for her, *sigh!* Little Heather, however, was not in the least daunted and didn't even look back to wave. Poor Mum! I had many friends there, and enjoyed learning, sports and even music lessons.

As there were few kids my age in my neighbourhood, I was, at times, lonely at home, my brothers being much older than me. That just served to make me quite self-reliant, and I learned to amuse myself.

Fortunately, I loved to read and spent many hours lost in stories and children's comics. Eventually as I grew up, I learned to love reading the English classics. I also played board games with my brothers when they had some spare time. It wasn't too often that I'd win, since they were much smarter than me. It did, however, serve to sharpen a competitive streak in me. Through the years, I strove to win or at least to excel in playing whatever game I could persuade them to play. Luckily for me, they adored their baby sister and humoured me often!

Throughout my childhood, religion or Christian faith meant little to me. Indeed, church had no place in our family life that I was aware of. I had asked my parents to take me to Sunday school when I was about eight, but I felt very out of place, and after only two weeks, I decided not to go back.

When I was twelve, a new girl—Diane—joined my class at school. She was different and started talking about Jesus and Christianity. The only time I had heard the name of Jesus, up to that point, was when it was used as a swear word at home. No one in the family ever went to church, unless to attend a wedding. And being a Christian? Well, of course I was a Christian because I was born in a Christian country, right?

At this point, I had little knowledge of who Jesus was and is. Neither did I have any idea of what being a Christian really meant. In fact, I used to think that Jesus was just a mythical figure, not a historical, real live person. Several of us used to argue with Diane about these things, and with hindsight, we really gave her a hard time. Finally, she invited us to come to her church, a local Baptist church. Since I had nothing better to do, I went and kept going with her for a number of weeks. You see, there was a hunger in my heart for God, a vague emptiness, though I hadn't realised it.

Slowly, I began to understand that Jesus was and still is the Son of God, and had come to earth with a mission; a purpose, and a plan to redeem mankind from the consequences of sin and disobedience to God. However, that gift of redemption has to be accepted—personally—or it is of no effect. One Sunday as the pastor was preaching, I realised that I was *not* a Christian and that I needed to accept Jesus as my personal Saviour. That night at the age of thirteen, I knelt beside my bed and asked Jesus to forgive my sins, and I chose, at that moment, to live my life for Him and not for myself any longer. There were many young people in my church, and I got involved in many of the activities that were going on. Life was indeed full and happy. My oldest brother, by this time, was working abroad and came home infrequently. My second brother was married and therefore had his own home. So, though I didn't have their company at home, I had many new friends at church.

However, troubled times lay ahead for our family. Two years later, my parents separated, and I found myself with my dad, a new stepmum, and stepsister. The challenges were many and, from the age of seventeen, I found myself neglecting—even ignoring—God as the pleasures of the world beckoned. Jesus was there for me, but I chose to turn my back on Him, and instead I went my own way. The great news is that even though we turn our backs on God *for a season*, He never turns His back on us—as I would later discover.

Through the tough times my mum had experienced, she had realised her need of a Saviour and had put her trust in Jesus Christ. She died when I was twenty-three and so went to be with Him in heaven. I found that a difficult time, as I had not been very close to her and thus regretted missed opportunities of knowing her better. With hindsight, it was a very hard, but good, lesson in not taking anyone for granted, not wasting time in life and making the most of every moment.

My dad and stepmum had moved up to Scotland to retire, and I went with them to begin my working career there. After a few years, in my late twenties, I found myself working in administration for the local government in the remote and beautiful Highlands of Scotland. I worked with an older lady who had a personal relationship with Jesus. Though she didn't say much to me about Him, I was reminded of my teenage years and how I had loved Him then. Upon securing a promotion at work that entailed moving to Inverness, the capital of the Highlands, I knew in my heart God was saying to me, 'Here is a new job, a new start in a new place. Won't you come back to Me?' I purposed in my heart that that is what I would do.

God is so gracious. When I finally found a small house to purchase, I discovered my neighbour was a Christian and attended the local Baptist church! I started to attend the church with him and got to know the believers there. When I asked God to take over my life for the second time, I knew this was for keeps—no going back. I had been in the world, known some of its pleasures, and decided that Jesus was more important than all of that. I wanted Him to be the Lord of all my life.

So, God lovingly and gently began the process of showing me the wrong and selfish attitudes and habits I'd acquired. By asking Him for strength and determination, I was able to replace these with compassion for others. Life was good once again. I had a peace I had not known for a very long time. I also had a good job, my own little house, and my own car. What more could I want?

I began to date a guy from church, the son of a former missionary family. He had grown up in southern Africa. I became interested in his life, having grown up in such a strange land, though it was difficult to relate to something I had not seen or experienced. After one year, he had to move away to find work, though we were sure God would somehow bring us back together. After another year of long-distance dating, our situations had not changed. We reluctantly realised that we should end our relationship. The parting was very painful for us both.

By this time, and after another promotion at work, I had a choice to consider. Should I leave work and study to get a university degree? Was there any chance God would want to use me somehow to serve Him? I remember that instead of asking God to bless the plans I wanted to make for my life, for the first time, I instead asked Him, 'What do *You* want me to do with my life?' I was willing to do what He wanted of me, but I thought I didn't have any skills to offer in serving Him full time. So, I began to think about studying. Where, what, and how do I pay for it?

Meantime, a guy named Chris from church was getting married to Ros, who hailed from Nottingham. When I met her for the first time, I liked her instantly. Her parents had been missionaries in former Zaire (now the Democratic Republic of Congo) some years back, and she had spent some of her childhood there. She was a Christian, as were her sisters. A group of their friends from our church, including me, drove down to Nottingham some months later for their wedding. It was a very joyful celebration. In talking with Ros's brother afterwards; he said something that struck me. He said, 'I'd love to work in a third-world country and help other people, but they won't have me because I'm not a Christian'. That stopped me dead in my tracks. I thought, 'I *am* a Christian, and I am willing, so what is to stop me from going?' The way his words struck me so forcibly was unusual, and I had a sense God was speaking to me through Ros's brother.

I did the only sensible thing to do, and that was to pray and ask God to confirm if that was really Him speaking to me. A week or so later, I was reading in Matthew's Gospel, chapter 9, verses 35–38:

> Jesus went through all the towns and villages, teaching in their synagogues, preaching the good news of the Kingdom and healing every disease and sickness. [36] When he saw the crowds, he had compassion on them, because they were harassed and helpless, like sheep without a shepherd. [37] Then he said to his disciples, 'The harvest is plentiful but the workers are few. [38] Ask the Lord of the harvest, therefore, to send out workers into his harvest field'.

I had heard sermons before on this passage of Scripture, but this time, the words seemed to jump out of the page at me, especially the challenge of the workers being so few. The next day, I opened my daily devotional book, and lo and behold, the Scripture for that day was Matthew 9:35–38. By this time, I was beginning to bubble with trepidation, excitement, and anticipation. The following day was Sunday, and in the evening service, we sang a song with the words:

> The fields are white unto harvest
> But O, the labourers are so few,
> So Lord I give myself to help the reaping,
> To gather precious souls unto You.
> Here I am, wholly available.
> As for me, I will serve the Lord.[1]

To me, this was unmistakably based on Matthew 9:35–38.

It could be no coincidence that the same passage of Scripture could come to my attention on each of three consecutive days. Now I *had* to take this seriously. What should I do next? I wondered and prayed. I went to Ros, my mature, now-married Christian friend whose counsel I valued. 'My problem is I think God is calling me to full-time service, but what skills do I have to offer?' I asked her.

'Missionary societies need administrators; even MAF needs administrators', she replied. Ros spoke emphatically, almost incredulously, that I should think I could be of no use! This was my introduction to the organisation Mission Aviation Fellowship. I remembered that Ros had worked for them prior to her marriage to Chris, but it had skipped my mind up to that point. So, we agreed to pray together for the Lord to continue to make His will plain to me, and I went to share with my pastor what I thought God was doing in my life.

He encouraged me to share this with the missionary core group in the church. These were a group of eight or so mature church members who had a particular interest in missionary

---

[1] Chris A Bowater, *Songs & Hymns of Fellowship Book 3*. Kingsway Publications 1987

work. Their role was to guide me and pray with me regarding the next steps to take. They asked about how I'd felt *called*— what had happened. Of course, they looked at my life to see if they could recommend me as an individual for missionary work. They committed to praying with me and encouraged me to consider where they Lord would have me serve.

I sent out letters of enquiry to three different mission organisations, but only one responded. It just so happened that this was Mission Aviation Fellowship! They enclosed a job description of a vacant position they had in Nairobi, Kenya. The job contained elements of all the jobs I had done during my working career, even when I was not walking with God. Truly I felt this was the Lord restoring to me the years that the locusts had eaten (see Joel 2:25a), in other words, the years I had spent living for myself and not for God. I duly completed the application form in September 1990 and had to wait patiently for it to be processed and for MAF to write for and obtain written references about me.

During this time, the doubts came. I wondered, 'What about my father and stepmother? They are not getting younger, and they depend on me for emotional support', In answer, I came across Jesus' words in Luke 14:26: '"If anyone comes to me and does not hate his father and mother, his wife and children, his brothers and sisters—yes, even his own life—he cannot be my disciple'.

Of course, I did not literally have to hate my relatives, but rather to put Jesus as first priority above all of them.

Then came the thoughts, *How will I manage to live? What about finances? Aren't missionaries poor and always asking for money?* Again, God answered the doubt with more of Jesus' teaching:

> And why do you worry about clothes? See how
> the lilies of the field grow. They do not labour
> or spin. ²⁹ Yet I tell you that not even Solomon
> in all his splendour was dressed like one of

these. ³⁰ If that is how God clothes the grass of the field, which is here today and tomorrow is thrown into the fire, will he not much more clothe you, O you of little faith? ³¹ So do not worry, saying, 'What shall we eat?' or 'What shall we drink?' or 'What shall we wear?' ³² For the pagans run after all these things, and your heavenly Father knows that you need them. ³³ But seek first his kingdom and his righteousness and all these things will be given to you as well. (Matthew 6:18–33)

Finally, one day in December, a church member was relating an experience he'd had when working as a missionary in Eire. One young man had come to join the church outreach team there and had to leave after six months. He couldn't handle living away from his home environment and culture. As I drove home after this conversation, I asked myself and mused over whether I was being carried away by my own enthusiasm. As I opened my front door, the phone was ringing. It was Ros, calling to chat.

At the end of the conversation, she said, 'Oh, by the way, I've been meaning to tell you for ages, but I kept forgetting. You remember at my wedding last July you sat at the table with my pastor and his wife?'

'Yes', I replied.

'Well, the pastor's wife mentioned that she'd had the strongest feeling, at that time, that God was calling you to the mission field'!

It was no coincidence—within thirty minutes of wondering whether or not God was really directing my steps, a confirmation came in such a direct way. Before going to sleep, I happened to read Psalm 139:2 that says: 'You know when I sit and when I rise; you perceive my thoughts from afar'.

That was the end to any doubt about my call, or about God's ability to look after me and the family members I would leave behind. I decided to obey Him and leave them in His tender care.

My application to MAF was being processed, and I started getting excited about the thought of living and working in Nairobi. However, one day, I stopped to think more deeply. 'Am I applying for a particular job, or am I applying to work with MAF and to go wherever I am needed?' I realised that, in fact, I was applying to work with MAF, and I would respond to whatever place I was most needed. It was just as well because by the time I went to the MAF headquarters for an interview in January 1991, the post in Nairobi had been filled. I was asked to consider either Uganda or Chad. After a little thought and a vague recollection that Chad was a hot and dusty place with lots of flies, I chose Uganda. I did not know much about the country and couldn't find out much up-to-date information. However, to Uganda I was headed!

My father and stepmother were not Christians. They could not understand why I would give up my job, my home, my car—in short, my whole life, as far as they were concerned—to go and 'work for charity', as my father put it. With hindsight, I think they felt I was deserting them and leaving them alone without any family support nearby. I was really torn but still felt I had to obey God's call and had to entrust my beloved parents to Him.

To encourage anyone else who is facing that same hard decision, my father gave his life to Jesus some years later, I believe as a consequence of my obedience to the call of God and in response to prayer for him.

CHAPTER 2

First Experience in Africa

On 2 June 1991, I arrived at the Entebbe International Airport, Uganda. I must admit, it looked rather rundown, and there were huge spiders with dirty, dangling cobwebs hanging from the flat roof. The ceiling was non-existent. Men in army uniforms carried guns. They were stationed in the *arrivals hall*, watching incoming passengers. I found all this a bit intimidating.

But what a relief—here was a familiar face! MAF pilot Ray had come to meet me. Since he had his pilot's uniform on, he could come to the airside of the airport. He helped me with immigration formalities and collecting my bags. I had met Ray, his wife Vi, and their toddler son, Jason, at MAF UK headquarters three weeks earlier. They were on their way out to Uganda, coming from their native Canada. I was so glad to see him!

Was Uganda what I expected? To be honest, I didn't have any prior expectations, so I can't say I was disappointed or that any expectations were fulfilled. It was so, so different from anything I had experienced before. I had visited several countries in Europe and had taken a holiday with my uncle and aunt in Bahrain when I was eight years old, but this was way different.

I took in my first sights and sounds of Uganda on the way from the airport. We had to stop at an army checkpoint on the way—the soldiers were gruff and unfriendly. They made me open every suitcase and even my guitar case, so they could look through my things. Did they think I was hiding guns or something? I was nervous, but Ray was quite matter of fact and just did as they asked. We moved on.

One thing that struck me was how green everything was—Uganda was obviously a fertile land and beautiful. Entebbe is on the shores of Lake Victoria. The water looked as blue as the sky, and the lake was so inviting—until I was told that I could get a worm infestation called bilharzia from swimming in the lake! The desire quickly faded, in spite of the heat and humidity of the late afternoon. I wondered how Ray managed to drive so confidently along the road. Fortunately, there wasn't much traffic. He had to weave from side to side, dodging potholes in the middle and avoiding the edges of the road that had been earlier washed away by rain. I later heard it said that only a drunk person drives in a straight line on Uganda's roads! Hmmm. I was mesmerised by all the new sights and sounds.

We arrived at Kampala, the capital city, about an hour later. The streets were not busy; I presumed because it was Sunday. Everything had a rundown look, from the paint peeling off buildings to the pockmarks in walls. I later discovered the holes in the walls were caused by flying bullets from Uganda's turbulent past. The roads had many potholes, and the drains were clogged with rubbish and red soil. Grass grew in every corner. I was to stay with Emil and Margrit for a few days till the renovations on my house were completed. It was good to be in a place where I could learn about aspects of my new life and ask questions (very many of them!). However, after ten days, I was ready to move into my own place and unpack my things, make new curtains, and generally make myself a new home.

All houses had iron bars on the windows and doors for security. The metal was bent into creative shapes to make them look less like a prison, but it still took time to get used to. I inherited two large dogs from Emil and Margrit when they left a month later, which I appreciated. They were outdoor guard dogs, but no one had told them they only had to bark at would-be thieves. They barked at everything and everyone in sight! I got used to it with time and hoped my neighbours did, too. Thankfully, I had a nice garden with colourful, exotic flowers of all shapes and sizes.

The house was interesting, to say the least. It had an upper story above the garage and this was my bedroom. Then began the battle with the bats—yes, bats. At least they were just the small type! The sloping roof above the bedroom was finished with corrugated iron sheets, but the builder had not sealed the spaces between the sheets and the top of the wall properly. Thus, bats had squeezed in the gaps and taken over the roof space. What was worse, they could squirm their way down a gap in the middle of the wall and get into my bedroom through the air vents in the wall. Of course, this only happened at night, since they all slept during the day.

I was thankful for having a mosquito net over my bed, which was tucked in under the mattress, so they couldn't get to me. But the noise of a bat flying around the bedroom invariably woke me up. With time, I discovered how to solve the problem. I would sit up in bed and wave my arms around. The movement kept the bat flying back and forth until it got tired and landed on the floor. Then I would quickly leap out of bed and hit it with my slipper until it died.

I apologise to any bat lovers reading this, but it was the only way to dispose of the invaders and get some sleep. They are regarded as vermin in Uganda and are numerous. I arrived when the weather was not too hot, but I discovered another problem with the bats as the weather warmed up—-the smell of the dung in the roof space! Eventually, the landlord agreed to have the roof space fumigated, the dung removed, and the roof space sealed. I was quite relieved.

My kind of house (with hot and cold running water and a flushing toilet) was for expatriates and those who could afford the relatively expensive monthly rent. Other kinds of houses, especially in the slum areas, were built of mud walls and had mud floors. Sometimes, the exterior walls had been rendered with cement to make them last longer and withstand the tropical rains. I felt comfortably at home within my four walls and felt as safe as I could.

I started working in the office very soon after my arrival. There was only one other staff member in the office, a Ugandan called Ruth. After Emil and Margrit left, the rest of the expatriate team consisted of two other families and me. Much as MAF provided an air transport service, I quickly learned that that was only one part of what we did. HF (or high frequency) radio was used to enable the office to maintain contact with our planes in the air for safety purposes. Twice daily we also used the radio to contact many upcountry mission stations, which were situated in remote areas of the country. We used to carry out many tasks for the missionaries that could only be done in Kampala, such as shopping for fresh vegetables, taking passports to the Immigration Department, and making airline bookings. You name it; if we could do something for anyone else, we would. Apart from that, I was responsible for ensuring that flights were booked properly and that the passengers paid for their flights. The office was busy, but the work was varied and gave me a great deal of satisfaction. I made many new friends amongst the missionary community, though nearly all served upcountry.

My new home (and the MAF office next door) was a two-minute walking distance from the local Baptist church. It soon became my new spiritual home. I quickly settled in and joined the discipleship and music ministries, as I had been involved in similar roles back home. There were a few expatriates in the church, but for the most part it was a Ugandan church. It was lively, and I really enjoyed the pastor's teaching ministry.

One thing I quickly learned is that Ugandans are not shy about talking about their faith or expressing their love for God as they worship Him. The prayer time during the service was often a time when everyone in the congregation would pray out loud, all at the same time. It was very confusing at first, so I had to train myself to switch off from the sounds 'round about me and mean my own business with God! The faith of the believers was very tangible—they had to trust God for everyday things that I used to take so much for granted. Food, shelter, money for transport and school fees—the list of needs seemed endless. I was learning valuable lessons from day one.

Contact with home was a major concern. We had no email then, and phone calls cost an equivalent of £12 per minute. I had to restrict phone calls home to Christmas, Mother's Day, Father's Day and birthdays—and even then only a very few minutes for each call. Letters took around two weeks to get to the UK, so I had to write frequently to let my folks know I was okay. The letters I received were always too short and infrequent for me but only because I was so eager to hear news from family and friends.

There were not many single expatriates that I knew in Kampala, and the few I did know, I knew through church. I didn't want to have only white friends, but I was discovering that it was so much easier to relate with those whose worldview and sense of humour were similar. This was my first introduction to cultural differences. Since I had not lived in, or been exposed to, a foreign culture for an extended period before, I had not been forced to think much about or understand my own culture. The immediate source of knowledge about the culture of the *Baganda* people living in and around Kampala was Ruth, my co-worker. She took great delight in sharing about her life and her customs. But I also began to realise that just as there were over fifty different tribes and languages in Uganda, so each of these had its own culture, too. Some were quite similar to each other, but others were very different. Would I ever figure it all out?

I had to realise that my way of thinking and doing things was not necessarily right, just different. Following that train of thought, I decided to learn all I could about Ugandan culture in general, so that I could understand the people better and perhaps learn to understand myself better, too. There were things in Ugandan culture that I could not agree with, but I also realised, perhaps for the first time, that some aspects of

15

my own culture were not that good, either. Because of differences in education, exposure to information about the world, and my different economic status, it was not so easy to form friendships with Ugandan girls. Mona was great fun, but she moved away from Kampala to study. Susan was with me in discipleship class, but when she asked me to lend her money, it put a barrier between us as I wondered about the basis of our relationship. I didn't want to impose myself on my MAF colleagues, as they had their own families to take care of. So, I stumbled on through my first year, struggling to have my social needs met. I was lonely at times, but it was easy at first, just to get immersed in work and forget that life had to be kept in balance. It took me six months to realise this, at which point I decided I had to make a life for myself outside of MAF.

I'd gotten to know a Canadian family by this point. They lived and worked in the west of Uganda, so they invited me to go and visit them for a week's holiday. Their house was a little rundown compared to mine, but then I realised it was a whole lot better than most of the housing in the town. There was electricity, but it was available only sporadically. That meant no fridge, no hot water—and no shower. Getting oneself clean consisted of running water in a plastic basin, placing it in the bathtub, throwing water over yourself, soaping and then rinsing. It was not for the fainthearted on a cold morning! I managed, though I admit I grumbled to myself.

At first, I wondered how on earth they managed to bring up their little girl in such an environment. Then I realised I'd been living a very sheltered kind of life and thanked God afresh for all the so-called luxuries that I enjoyed and took for granted, living in the city. I soon discovered that it is fairly easy to do without electricity, but if you have no water, that is unbearable. I rubbed my hands in glee when the City Council Roads Department decided to grade the side road leading to the MAF office and my house. The road sloped downhill and was very badly rutted all the way down, and there were no drains either side of the road to take the storm water when it rained. In fact, some ruts were more like gullies and had to be driven over slowly and cautiously to avoid the grinding crunch of hitting the underside of the car on the bumps. So, we all looked forward to being able to drive comfortably from the main road down to our gates. The problem was that the water main ran just under the surface of the road, and the driver of the grading machine hadn't bothered to check the city water supply maps (if indeed there was such a thing).

So, the water pipe was fractured as the grader did its work, and water started gushing down the newly-graded road, creating—you guessed it—another gully! It was like the game *Snakes and Ladders*. Grade the road? Up the ladder! Burst the water main? Down an even longer snake. Thankfully, I had a mains water storage tank to supply my house, but it wasn't actually that big. *How long would it last*, I wondered? How long would it need to last?

Fortunately for me, the house next door—the one that housed the MAF office—had huge rainwater storage tanks that were fed from the guttering of the house, so I was able to use that water. My maid used to carry twenty-litre jerry cans of water from the tanks to my house every day. By flushing my toilet only once a day, I was able to eke out the supply in my mains water tank and so managed to survive the three months it took the water department to repair the burst main. Never again did I take a supply of fresh water for granted, and even now I dread any time the water supply stops for any reason.

Life was full of adventures: new people, new experiences, and new places. I took part in leading a discipleship class, and I even led the church choir for a time! I discovered many new and interesting things about life and about myself. Sometimes, I had to laugh long and hard at myself, especially, for example, the time I managed to get the MAF *Land Rover* stuck in the mud. How on earth can you get a Land Rover stuck? You may well wonder, but it was really very easy.

CHAPTER 3

Life in Uganda

Whether or not to have someone working for you, either in the house or looking after the garden, is a question all foreigners face when living in developing countries. It can sound *frightfully colonial* to say you have a maid or house-girl! However, I decided that since most Ugandans had someone working for them, and since I could give someone an income by employing them, I ended up having a house girl and *shamba* boy (shamba means garden).

So, Fred was the guy who worked in my garden, keeping the grass cut and tending the flowers. That was his daytime Monday to Saturday job, but on Sunday he preached in a local vernacular (or Luganda-speaking) church. In fact, he was the pastor, Pastor Fred.

One day, he came with a suggestion for a mission. He wanted to go with a team from his church to preach in a certain village outside of Kampala. However, they didn't have transport. But I did, in the form of the MAF Land Rover! It could seat nine at a squeeze, and so it came about that I became a member of their missions team—well, just the transport provider and driver—but we would go out once a month to encourage believers in small rural churches and preach and teach about Jesus.

Roads in rural areas were, of course, made of dirt—*murram*, to be precise. This is a kind of clay soil that is quite rocky and so makes a good road bed as it packs really hard over time. I hadn't had much experience driving on dirt roads, but I figured that driving in icy, snowy conditions in Scotland should stand me in good stead.

However, I didn't know that murram can be a very difficult surface to drive on when the road has been newly-graded. It was especially tricky if it had not been well-compacted with a road roller and then it is rained on. The surface becomes very loose and *very* slippery. The other interesting fact is that when a road is graded, it has quite a noticeable camber to it, so that rainwater runs off to the sides and doesn't affect the road surface in the middle.

Putting all these facts together, one cloudy day we had gone out for a mission. The village church was quite a few kilometres off the main tarmac road, but that was okay because the road had been newly graded and was like a highway. The way there was great; the way back home was a bit different. It had rained heavily, and the road surface had become *very* slippery. However, I stuck to the 'tramlines' other vehicles' tyres had made in the middle of the road. We moved along slowly, singing praises to God for the successful mission and for those who had given their lives to Jesus that day.

The Land Rover was seriously overloaded with passengers at this point. I am very strict on obeying the law and driving responsibly. However, I hadn't realised that, to a Ugandan, a vehicle is not full unless you simply can't squeeze anyone else in! In addition to the members of our missions team, other believers had asked for a free lift back to the city. I hadn't known what was going on since they all spoke Luganda. My gardener-cum-pastor didn't think it would be a problem. So, our team had gotten into the vehicle first, then others just kept piling in. I think there were an extra four inside before I realised what was happening. By the time I asked Fred what was going on, even more were trying to squeeze their rear ends in to get the door shut! At least I was able to stop more from getting in, but it was impossible to get the extra passengers out. I told Fred we could take them to the main road, but no further as I was breaking the law. I know he did not understand my reasoning. We continued with the windscreen gradually steaming up due to so many hot, sweaty bodies in close proximity and their clothes still damp from the earlier rain.

The problem came when we met an oncoming vehicle. Since I had the big four-wheel drive Land Rover, I courteously pulled over a little to the side of the road to allow the other vehicle to pass. However, the other driver knew exactly what he was doing and stayed right in the middle, or on the crown of the road. With the additional weight of people inside the car, we slid gently sideways and downwards as I tried to inch slowly forwards and upwards to get back on to the crown of the road. We came to rest with the side of the vehicle firmly embedded in the small bank at the road-side. I tried forward and reverse gears, but we were well and truly stuck. We were also in the middle of nowhere, or so it seemed to me. Everybody piled out and stood watching, waiting for me to fix the problem.

I am usually good at problem-solving, but I was just as firmly stuck as the Land Rover was with this one. I was worried about being in the *back of beyond* late in the afternoon. I was annoyed with myself for getting stuck in the mud. And I was still mad at the number of people that had piled into the vehicle against my wishes (and against the law, don't forget!). Plus, I felt totally helpless in the situation.

When the team realised I couldn't get us out of the mess we were in, Ugandan creativity and ingenuity rose to the fore! The team actually *pushed* the vehicle from the side that was stuck, as if trying to push it sideways. This was just enough help to allow the vehicle to move forward in a low gear with low revs! We slowly inched out of the gully at the side of the road and got traction on the (by now) drying and hardening road surface. *Whew!* We all cheered and sang and shouted praise to God for our deliverance. And I learned many lessons about driving a vehicle and driving passengers that day, too.

One of the team, Moses, was musical and would write vernacular songs. The team consisted of young men and women who had lovely voices, and so it came about that in addition to driving the Land Rover, I played my guitar to accompany their original music. Since I am no great guitar player, it was just as well that nearly all the songs had a very simple melody that required only three, or at most, four different chords. I even learned some of the words so that I could sing along, too, much to the initial amazement and amusement of the listeners.

Through these interesting excursions, I learned the value of teamwork and complementary skills and gifts. I couldn't speak Luganda, much less share my faith with non-English speaking Baganda people, but I could help others to do so. The team was not able to travel to some of the village areas to preach and teach, but through me and the faithful MAF Land Rover, they were able to go to villages and share the love of Jesus in a powerful and life-transforming way. When we added the accompaniment of the guitar, we shared the Gospel in song in a way that touched people deeply. All in all, I believe I, too, will get some of the credit in heaven for the numbers who gave their hearts and lives to Jesus through these outreaches, even though I said not a word.

CHAPTER 4

Joy Grindey, the Unsung Missionary Heroine

During my first year in Uganda, I met a very interesting older lady. She had been in Uganda for more than thirty-five years, working with Africa Inland Mission, assisting in Bible translation work in the northwest of the country. As a young twenty-five-year-old woman, she had left England just after the Second World War to come to Africa and help translate the Bible into some local languages in Uganda. She had never married but had dedicated her life to serving her Saviour. I admired her commitment so much. In spite of the length of time she had been away from her home country, Joy was very *English*. Her accent, her very proper use of language, and her sense of humour were all very English. We took a liking to each other, and whenever she was in Kampala, she would stay in my spare room. In due course, she invited me to come and spend a short holiday with her.

'I have a guest cottage', she said. 'You'll have a wonderful time ... do come'!

Since MAF flew to the town of Arua almost daily, I was able to fly up to see her, thus avoiding a terrifying twelve-hour bus journey there and back. Not only were the buses rather dilapidated, the road was riddled with potholes. To cap it all, there were periodic attacks on vehicles by armed thugs. So, I enjoyed the ninety-minute flight. The pilot pointed out the

River Nile below us, Lake Albert to the left, and the spectacular Murchison Falls just before the Nile entered the top of Lake Albert and continued north to Sudan. I had the navigation maps on my knee (when the pilot didn't need them) and enjoyed trying to figure out exactly where we were along the way.

Joy was there to meet me, and the first thing we did was to change our plans for the day! Two visitors had come from the UK to visit Archdeacon Henry Orombi, (who, over the years, became the archbishop of Church of Uganda). The archdeacon lived a two-hour drive away. He had been unable to come and meet the guests, so we all piled into Joy's ancient but faithful Daihatsu, and off we went. The vehicle had its original 'air-conditioning', that is, we drove with the windows wide open. I was really enjoying the sights of a part of Uganda I had not seen before. Even the dirt road was a light clay colour, instead of the red murram of the Kampala area.

A sudden flurry of activity from Joy got my attention, and I saw she was winding her window up fast and furiously while closing the two open vents on the dashboard. I wondered what was going on and what I should be doing when I noticed a large lorry coming towards us on the dirt road. All you could see was the cab of the lorry and then a cloud of pale dust it stirred up as it drove, obliterating the back of the lorry from view. Dust cloud! I tried to wind my window up as fast as I could but couldn't quite make it in time and a flurry of dust particles swept in and covered everything in sight. That was mostly me, as I was closest to the almost-closed window. I kept better watch for oncoming traffic after that and didn't get caught again!

After a couple of bone-shaking hours of driving, we arrived at our destination. We were shown to the sitting room and we waited and listened to the plans the visitors had for ministry with Rev Orombi. After some time, lunch was served for us. I was learning about African hospitality. Even though we were not expected, whatever food was being prepared for their lunch was shared with us.

Since food is cheap—after all, it is the sweat of your hands that makes it grow to harvest—then that is one thing for sure that can be prepared and shared with whoever happens to drop by. I realised that was so very different from my upbringing, where it is considered impolite to visit someone at mealtime. That is because only enough food is prepared for the number of people who are going to eat, with little or none to spare. In Africa, it is impolite *not* to share your food with others. That took me some time to understand and adopt, but gradually I saw the joy and benefit of having a *fellowship* meal with company while you eat, whether expected or not!

After a delicious lunch of beans and sweet potatoes, we headed off back to Kuluva Hospital where Joy lived. Kuluva was a mission hospital, and MAF had the privilege of serving the other missionaries and staff that worked there. Joy's home was small but comfortable and homey. It was made of mud bricks that had been rendered on the outside and inside with cement. It had the usual smooth cement floor, tastefully covered with woven grass mats. From the flowery curtains to the ornaments on the bookshelf, I could see this was really a home. My holiday was to be a lesson in how to live without electricity.

My guest room was actually more like a traditional mud hut, though it was rectangular. It had a low door that I had to duck under to pass through, and I could see the straight wooden tree branches that had been used for the roof trusses. Above that was grass-thatched roof. My bed had a rectangular bamboo frame hanging above it, and to this the mosquito net was tied. Neat job, I thought. I was glad of the mosquito net that night. As soon as I'd blown out the candle to go to sleep, I heard the very familiar noise of a bat flying around the room. Well, I sure wasn't going to get out of my safe haven behind the net to try and catch a bat in the dark or by torchlight! I decided to ignore it. A little later, I heard the sound of rustling coming from the grass thatch. I lay in the dark, wondering what on earth it could be. Needless to say, I didn't sleep too much that first night, but with time I learned to ignore the noises and sleep anyway.

Joy had a very interesting hot-water system in her house. Each afternoon, her house-girl brought firewood. She climbed a small ladder holding a jerry can, and poured the water into an old oil drum that lay on its side, supported on a brick frame at a height of about two metres. She then lit a fire under the oil drum, which had pipes coming out of it that then went through the wall into Joy's bathroom! It was an ingenious system, with hot water supplied directly to the bathtub! Interestingly, the water smelled of wood smoke, but to have a warm bath at the cool end of a hot and dusty day was a lovely treat.

Though there was a bathtub and wash hand basin in the bathroom, the toilet was outside. But even the toilet had a special touch! It was the first long-drop I had seen where a makeshift toilet pan had been built up to accommodate the toilet seat. It was a real toilet with improved ventilation, so there were no smells—a real VIP toilet!

Joy loved to have papaya with buttered toast and marmalade for breakfast each day.

'Now how do you prepare toast without an electric toaster?' I asked myself.

Since necessity is the mother of invention, there was a solution! Joy had a small metal frame on which slices of toast could be placed above the flame on the gas cooker. They were at just the right angle to get toasted without being burned. And what about butter for the toast, since there was nowhere to buy any and no fridge to keep it fresh? Joy had taught the house-girl how to make butter from the cream on the top of the milk, and so she would make a small quantity from time to time. It could keep for those few days until it was used up. That was a real treat for me as I had to make do with margarine in Kampala!

Another thing that I found interesting was the cupboard that was used for food storage. It was just a cupboard on legs but it had opening doors that were covered with a fine wire mesh. Under each leg, there was a container like the lid of a jar, filled with cooking oil. The oil stopped the ever-present ants (of a variety of shapes and sizes) from climbing up the legs to access whatever was stored in the 'larder'. Then the fine mesh kept out even the smallest fruit flies, so whatever was in the larder stayed fresh and bug-free!

Joy lived a simple life, without many 'mod cons', but she had adapted herself so that she could have what, to her, were the essentials of life, without living in luxury. Small touches here and there made her life very comfortable, and I could see how she enjoyed living in a rural area, away from the stress of life in the city. I really enjoyed my rest and relaxation whilst staying with her.

We took a trip into Arua one day, and she introduced me to Solomon. He had been carrying bags of cement for a building project he was undertaking, and as she introduced us, he apologised and said, 'I'm so dirty; I am white from head to toe'. I tried hard not to laugh out loud at this, as he might have thought I was laughing at him. But how funny his statement was! I would have said, 'I'm so dirty; I am black from head to toe', but for an African, being white (or dusty) was equated with being dirty. I had to do a mental shift on that one, and I have never forgotten his hilarious statement.

From Joy's example, I learned that I could remain British but still adapt to Ugandan culture. Indeed, I can *never* be Ugandan—even if I am fluent in the local language, even if I adopt the local dress, and even if I marry a Ugandan. My roots cannot change, my origins cannot change because what has made me British in the first place cannot change. That helped me to understand where I came from and how it differs from the country in which I was now living and working. It also helped me to understand the process of adaptation to Ugandan culture—what I could adapt to and what I could not, or what was an unreasonable expectation in terms of adjustment. So much for the first impressions of my new life. It was very far removed from what I had known before, but through each new experience I was learning, growing and being stretched.

After fifteen months in Uganda, I went on holiday to South Africa to visit the guy from my church in Inverness whom I had dated for two years. I experienced something I had read about in books before I came to Uganda, and that is 'reverse culture shock'. This is when you return to your own (or similar) culture and instead of being shocked by the *lack* of goods and services, you are shocked by the *abundance* of these things. We stopped at a petrol station and decided to get a soft drink. There must have been around eight refrigerated cabinets *full* of all types of cans and bottles of drinks! I just stood and looked, paralysed by the amount of choice and had to leave the buying to my friend. I walked out and back to the car.

I adjusted quickly, however, and had a great holiday, but I realised that as a Christian, I had moved on. The man I thought could have been Mr. Right was, now, clearly not the man for the woman I had become. I came back to Uganda, vowing to serve God wholeheartedly as a single woman and to forget about relationships and marriage.

CHAPTER 5

The KPC Introduction

Three weeks later, Kampala Pentecostal Church (KPC) was holding its annual youth camp at a retreat centre some twenty miles from Kampala. Youth from several other churches were invited to attend, and some of my friends were going. I had decided not to stay at the three-day camp as it was a really busy time at work, and I had to finish my end of financial year reports before I could go anywhere.

So, I arrived midmorning on Saturday to find no spare seats among the young people who were gathered under the shade of a mango tree to listen to the guest speaker. A young lady, Maureen, offered me half of the table she was sitting on, so that became my perch for the rest of the session. The guest speaker was talking about the call of God in a person's life and how God guides and directs His children. He described exactly the process I had experienced—a rhema word that 'speaks' to your heart, confirmation through relevant portions in the Bible, wise counsel from godly men and women, and circumstances lining up to lead and direct your path. I contributed to the discussion as it so clearly outlined how God had led me to Uganda.

At lunchtime, Maureen, one of the young girls involved in the youth ministries took me under her wing and introduced me to her youth pastor, Chris. My first impression was that he was good looking, but I paid no further attention. The next day, I went to talk to the visiting guest speaker who was standing with Pastor Chris. To my surprise, I heard the words, *'He is the one for you'* quite distinctly. They were not audible words but were still unmistakable and referring to Pastor Chris. However, I didn't take it seriously, as I had just told God how I was in Uganda to serve Him and Him alone!

By chance, Pastor Chris's cousin, whom I had met previously at a Bible study group, asked me if I could give Chris a lift back home after the camp. I was the only one with a car, since everyone else had come by hired bus. I had no problem with that, so I ended up with Pastor Chris and a couple of others in my car, giving them a lift to the city. Since it turned out that he lived about a kilometre from my house, he was the last one to be dropped off. Considering that Chris and I had never met before in the first fifteen months of my stay in Uganda, the number of times we came into contact with each other during the ensuing weeks was amazing. At the youth camp, I'd met a girl from Wales, who came to Uganda to find out the church's response to the AIDS pandemic and was working with a local Christian non-government organisation called ACET (Aids Care, Education and Training). I had also given her a lift to town after the camp, and on hearing that she was staying in a Guest House, I extended an offer for her to come and stay in my spare room for the time she was in Uganda. She gladly accepted, and so I had company for a couple of months.

She attended KPC and invited me to some KPC youth events during this time. One Sunday, all the youth went to the youth pastor's home for a fun afternoon and to celebrate his soon-coming birthday. When she discovered that his birthday was in fact the next day, she invited him to come to my house to celebrate with a birthday dinner in his honour! All such meetings were unplanned as far as I was concerned, and it was like God was making our paths cross. I thought of Chris as a wonderful man of God, someone I respected enormously, and he was fun to be with.

He invited me to accompany him to an overnight prayer meeting—a first for me. I wondered how people could pray the whole night and not be bored or fall asleep. I soon found out that the night's activities had structured times of prayer, praise, and worship and preaching of the Word. So, I discovered that it was a great experience. I thought he had asked me so that I could give him a lift there and back. Again, he asked me to attend an event that turned out to be an important function with him. Again, I assumed it was so that I could give him a lift! I also asked him to come with me to a wedding in a town about three hours from Kampala. I thought he might like the trip out of town. Since we lived a mere 300 metres from each other, he would drop by to visit once or twice a week, and I would go and visit him too.

I was trying to be strictly friendly with Chris, though I had to admit he was a very nice person, and I really enjoyed his company and looked forward to the time we spent together. At Christmas time, he bought me a gift of a beautiful African dress, and I really loved it. I had no idea at that point of the significance of the gift, but in Uganda, by the time a guy buys a girl a dress, it means he is very serious about her! In blissful ignorance, I thought we were still just friends. It wasn't until we were praying together a couple of days later that Chris prayed, 'And Lord, I ask You to guide us in this relationship that we are beginning ...'

Relationship? I thought. *I didn't know we had a relationship*!

Of course, that led to a discussion of our friendship and how it had become something deeper. I had a peace about our relationship and felt that God was the One bringing us together. You have read my story, but now you must hear Chris's story and learn how he came to this point in his life.

CHAPTER 6

Chris's Family Background

C hris's family background is as different to mine as it is possible to get. His father, as was common with many African men at that time, had taken more than one wife. His first wife, whom he married in church in the 1920s, had a baby girl, a baby boy, and then continued to have more girls. Boys are valuable to an African family, as they get married and stay in the family home. Girls on the other hand marry into another man's family and so leave.

Boys are therefore necessary to carry on the family line. Girls, however, are needed as their future spouse has to give their family cows by way of a dowry. These cows are needed so that the boys can pay a dowry for the girls they will marry. It is therefore important to have a good balance of boys and girls to keep everybody happy. The concept of gender balance is by no means a new one!

With Chris's dad (known affectionately as Baba) having, at that point, many girls and only one boy from his first wife, the clan leaders told him he needed a second wife. So, he married again in a traditional ceremony. His new bride began to have children—girls again! So, he had to marry a third wife, who also began to bear girls. The fourth wife was brought and also began to bear girls. In fact, the second wife had five girls, Chris's mum had four girls and the fourth wife had three girls before Chris came on the scene as the second born son to his father! Imagine having fathered the first sixteen or so children and only two of them boys!

Just for the record, each of Baba's four wives had ten children, with the final tally being thirty-two girls and eight boys. Of course, the great irony is that it is the *man* who determines the sex of the child, *not the woman!* But that was not understood at that time, and the ladies had to take the 'blame' for not bearing enough sons.

Since the last three wives all lived together under one (very large) roof, Chris grew up in the midst of hustle, bustle, and noise. The wives got on well together, and consequently, all the children grew up as brothers and sisters with little distinction between them.

However, being the only boy for a long time in the communal home meant special treatment for Chris. He spent more time with his dad and mum and was fussed over by all his sisters. He was given *Okeny* as one of his middle names, meaning *'the boy who follows many girls'*. Despite the extra attention, he was a sickly child. He had contracted measles at the age of two and developed pneumonia afterwards as a result of an untreated cough. This caused damage to the lining of his lungs, though no one realised it at the time. His mother spent a lot of time and money taking him for various medical treatments and even to the local witchdoctor. The doctors diagnosed asthmatic bronchitis, but nothing improved his health. Consequently, he started school a year later than his peers and had to struggle with feeling unwell for a lot of the time.

As if that wasn't enough of a risk to his life, he also had his share of life-threatening accidents. One day, Baba was burning the long grass around the home to make a fire break for protection against the wildfires that can happen and cause havoc in the dry, windy season. He didn't know his toddler son had followed him to the field. Little Christopher was suddenly surrounded by burning grass, and his sweater caught fire. Thankfully, someone heard his screams, and he was rescued in the nick of time, miraculously without any major burns to his body.

As a young boy, he would go every day to the local river to bathe and play with his friends. One day, he was swept away by the strong current of the swollen river and was quickly carried downstream and out of sight. He couldn't swim but somehow managed to stay afloat and grab a branch that was hanging over the swirling waters. He was eventually dragged to the bank and to safety. I should add that the river is also home to crocodiles and hippos. Thankfully, they were not around at the time.

At nine years of age, a teacher who was a born-again Christian came to preach at the local church. He preached a simple message of salvation, and Chris gave his life to Jesus at that time. However, the local minister thought he was bringing a new religion to the church and told Chris to stop talking or thinking about salvation. Sadly, this led Chris to give up following Jesus for a time. Interestingly, the Christian teacher was the very same Henry Orombi, the archdeacon I later met in Arua and who later served as the archbishop of the Church of Uganda!

Another life-threatening incident with water happened at the secondary boarding school. By now Chris could swim, and he and some friends decided to go swimming at the local dam. In fact, they decided to swim from one side to the other. Since they were stronger swimmers than Chris, they quickly left him behind. About halfway across, he suddenly realised how exhausted he was. He couldn't go any further! However, it was either continue swimming or drown, so somehow he found the extra strength to make it to the other side. After dragging himself onto the shore, it took a good half hour before he could make his wobbly legs carry him back to the school.

It was while he was attending this school that he recommitted his life to Jesus through the influence of Scripture Union, a Christian group that met regularly at school for Bible study and prayer. He was the first in his family to accept Jesus as his personal Saviour and wasted no time in sharing his newfound faith with the rest of the family. Chris came to stay with his older sister in Kampala for his 'A' level exams and continued to follow Jesus. He decided to attend a new church that was being started in the city by a young Canadian missionary couple, Gary and Marilyn Skinner, on 22 April, Easter Sunday 1984. It was Kampala Pentecostal Church (KPC). He was one of the seventy-five people who met for the very first KPC service.

A miracle happened that same year when God healed Chris of the asthmatic bronchitis at a crusade held in Kampala by the late American preacher evangelist T. L. Osborn. How could Chris *not* share the Good News about Jesus with his family? Baba, however, was a religious man and was offended that his son was telling him that his religion was not enough and that he needed a personal relationship with God through Jesus! When Chris and his good friend Milton went home in 1985 to visit the family, Baba refused to accept the Bible that Chris brought him, saying that he could no longer see to read the fine print.

They asked if they could pray for Baba so that God could restore his sight. He agreed, though wondering what good it would do. God is so gracious! As Baba opened his eyes after the prayer and picked up the Bible, he realised he could read clearly! God had healed his sight! In fact, Baba could see to read his Bible until the day he died in January 1997 at the ripe old age of ninety-one years. Imagine the impact on Chris's family—two miracles of healing! Family members began to give their lives to Jesus until most of the family had become born-again Christians.

After the 'A' level examinations, Chris had qualified to study at the then prestigious and only university in the country, the Makerere University in Kampala. However, he felt God telling him to leave his studies and work as a volunteer in the church— which, at the time, was meeting in a former movie theatre. His sister and some other relatives were very angry at this decision. But Chris heeded the call of God and became the church's sound man, cleaner, security guard, a leader in their fledgling youth ministry and, generally, a jack of all trades in this growing church. This was unpaid work at first, but God provided for Chris's needs through the love and generosity of other church members. This was a time when he learned humility and how to serve others.

Soon, he was sensing that God had placed a call on his life; a call to work full time to serve Him in pastoral work. But how was he to get the necessary training? He continued to pray. In 1987, a Canadian team came to the church to minister. Out of the blue, one of the men on the team told him that God had said he should sponsor Chris to study at Pan Africa Christian College (PACC) in Nairobi for his theological training! This was not because the man was wealthy, but he paid the fees through self-sacrifice and because of his commitment to heed the voice of God.

So, in 1988, Chris began working toward his Bachelor of Arts in Bible Theology. He remained in Nairobi, except for some holidays, until he graduated in 1991. During his time at PACC, he was challenged about his surname, which was Komaketch. In Luo culture, children were given surnames with a bad or unlucky meaning in order to supposedly bring *good luck* in life. If a child was given a good name at birth, then it was thought that the good name would bring bad luck in later life! The extended family group, or clan, has a number of names that are unique to that particular clan, so a child is given a surname that is one of the clan names. Thus, the children born to one couple may each have a different last name—very interesting!

Chris's name Komaketch actually means, *'the cursed or unfortunate one'.* A fellow student asked him how he could be a pastor preaching the Good News about Jesus with a name like that? So, he changed his name to the made-up name of Komagum, which means 'the blessed or fortunate one'. In fact, he subsequently changed his name officially by deed poll just before we got married. I didn't want to be called Mrs. Cursed One, thank you very much!

Pastor Gary Skinner had asked Chris to come back to Kampala after his studies and become the first youth pastor at KPC. So, on Sunday, 2 June 1991, the very day I arrived in Kampala, Chris was formally inducted as pastor to the youth. His life was busy, and ministry was challenging but fulfilling. Above all, the youth were flocking to the church to follow Jesus and find direction and purpose in life. He went with a youth team to the far southwest of Uganda for a mission in early 1992. God moved in a mighty way, and miracles of healing took place, and many gave their lives to Jesus. However, there was also an outbreak of bacterial meningitis in that area. Within two weeks of his return to Kampala, Chris was in a coma in hospital, fighting for his life. Some things that happen in life are not easily understood at the time, and this was surely one of those.

After three days, there were five other men admitted to the same ward, all with meningitis. Those five men had died. Chris, however, regained consciousness only to discover he was paralysed.

'Is this what I studied three years at PACC for?' he asked God. *'If you heal me, I will dedicate my life to telling people about You and how You are the God who heals'.*

Thus began the slow process of Chris learning to sit up, to feed himself, and eventually to walk again. In fact, he had to use a wheelchair at first, then a Zimmer frame, then crutches, tripod sticks, and finally an ordinary walking stick. By the time we met some seven months after the hospital admission, he was managing with the walking stick, so the recovery was long but assisted by thrice weekly physiotherapy sessions.

Prior to this, Chris had been one of the most eligible bachelors in the church! He had several girls who were seeking his company or asking to help him—in order to get his attention—but he remained aloof and prayerful. However, during the time of his recuperation, all these girls who had previously been showing interest in their youth pastor as a potential husband had faded away. Chris told God that he was not interested in any relationship leading to marriage until he was completely healed. Some few weeks later in October 1992, Pastor Chris took the youth for their annual youth camp.

He noticed the late arrival of a certain white lady on the Saturday morning of the camp and realised from her contribution to the discussions that she had the call of God on her life. A voice said to him, 'What about that one?' The voice meant as a *future wife*. He decided that it must be the devil trying to distract him from his calling and discarded the thought. He had thought no more of marrying a white missionary than I had of marrying an African pastor, but God had other plans for us both.

CHAPTER 7

Experiencing the Ugandan Culture

In the meantime, MAF had requested that I move to another house, from an apartment to a small bungalow with a garden. I didn't mind and found myself living a mere 300 metres from Chris! It wasn't a deliberate decision to move me nearer to Chris, but it was just a cheaper house to rent. I didn't mind—it meant we could walk to each other's house to visit. I liked my new home, but since I had moved to a different part of the city, I had to employ a new *shamba* boy. Pastor Fred continued to work for the lady who had rented my former house, and he recommended one of his church members to come and work for me. Philly's English was a bit limited to start with, as I soon discovered, but he was a hard-working and helpful young man.

I came home one evening and hadn't organised anything to eat, so I asked him to go and buy potatoes and flour. The local shop wasn't far, and he quickly came back with sweet potatoes and maize flour. He could see I wasn't so pleased to see what he had brought, but I had to admit it was my mistake for not making things clear. So, I reassured him and rearranged what I had planned to eat. From then on, I was careful to specify carefully what I meant. In this case, I should have said I wanted *Irish* potatoes and *wheat* flour. Point noted!

In the new house, I had been hearing scuffling noises coming from the ceiling. It had started above the kitchen.

After a week or so, the sounds moved above the dining room, next to the kitchen. From there the noises moved to the sitting room and eventually above my bedroom. At this point, I decided enough was enough and something had to be done. Whatever it was did not have my permission to disturb my sleep at night! I asked Philly to buy a rat trap, as I thought that was the most likely cause of the noise. So, he climbed into the roof space and set the trap. We caught nothing, and the noises continued. I finally had to ask him to crawl through the roof space to see if he could see what was making the scuffling sounds up there.

That evening when I came home, he said he had discovered what was disturbing me. Trying to explain and find the right word for whatever it was proved a challenge, however. In Luganda, the letter *k* followed by either *e*, *i*, or *y* is pronounced 'ch'. If it followed by either *a*, *o* or *u*, it is pronounced 'k'. So, the word *kitchen,* in English, can be quite a challenge to a Muganda trying to learn the language. Similarly, *chicken* is also a difficult word—bearing in mind that Philly had mostly learned how to *speak* the English he knew. He hardly knew how to read or write it. So, he stumbled for words and from what I could understand from him, I had a chicken in my roof space. How on earth it got there was a complete mystery. I asked him to climb back up there the next day and catch the offending creature. How he was going to do that, I left to his own ingenuity.

I came home in the evening, musing over what I would do with a chicken. Would it be big enough to eat? If not, where could I keep it (that my dog couldn't get to) to fatten it up? Had Philly even been able to catch the chicken, or would he simply have been able to chase it out through whatever hole it had come in through? As I parked the car, he told me to be careful when I opened the door because the chicken was in the kitchen, and I shouldn't let the dog in. Picturing a chicken strutting around my kitchen, I was just hoping he had put it somewhere where it couldn't make a mess. Fancy leaving the chicken in the kitchen. *Why not put it in the garage?* I thought.

However, a surprise was in store. There was a cardboard box in the kitchen, and when I looked in, to my complete surprise, there were two *kittens*. I laughed as I realised how Philly had struggled to say the right word for what he had found. But then, what was I going to do with these tiny cute bundles of fur that looked like they were not even old enough to be weaned? What about the mother cat—where was she?

Philly had found the hole in the roof space where the mother cat had got in, and he blocked it up. Since the mother was nowhere in sight, I was now stuck with two kittens when I already had a large dog that could and would eat these creatures in one gulp. At least when milk was put down in a saucer and the kittens got used to the taste, they would lap the milk up greedily, so feeding wasn't a problem. An improvised cat litter tray solved the toilet issue. Still, I had to keep them out of the way of the dog, who was very excited by the new animal smell. And I didn't particularly like cats.

As they grew and gained confidence, I had to laugh at their antics in the kitchen. They climbed and fell over the basket that was their bed and chased each other around. Over and through the legs of the kitchen stools they went, climbing in and out of a clay pot that I had put on the floor for them to play with, and they were always wrestling with each other. They seemed to like playing a game of rugby, tackling each other when the other one least expected it. I had a lot of laughs just watching them, and yes, I even enjoyed playing with them, too.

Growing kittens need space, and I couldn't keep them in the kitchen forever. What was I going to do with them? Chris came to my rescue, at this point, and said he would be glad to have them. Problem solved! And I would still get to see them at his house. My dog, who had been somewhat excluded from my house because of the kittens, was now allowed access again, so he was very happy to see them go. I don't like attributing largely human qualities to animals, but I could swear he had been a teensy-weensy bit jealous of them.

During that time, Chris and I kept meeting each other, and we eventually started visiting each other at home. He started sending out signals to tell me that he was interested in me. I, however, was totally oblivious to this. His *signals* were not the same signals that I was used to in my culture, so I assumed he was just being friendly. It is only when you get to know a culture intimately that such things would be understood. For him, he knew we had a relationship forming. For me, I had no idea until the prayer time we had together just after Christmas Day 1992.

CHAPTER 8

The Cross-Cultural Dating Experience

As Chris and I were getting to know each other, a cultural difference crept in here. At this time, there was no practice of 'dating' amongst the Christian youth of Uganda then. Rather than relying on *sparks of excitement* or attraction when looking for a potential life partner, a serious Christian man seeking a wife would study the woman's character, her family's upbringing, and her degree of commitment to her personal faith. Then he would spend time getting to know her by sharing a soda or coffee, or chatting after church.

Only when they both liked each other thus far, would they talk of dating—with a view to marriage. A Ugandan woman would not dream of dating a guy that she could not at some point see herself marrying. Assuming they continued relating well, love for each other would then begin to grow. However, the relationship would not get physical; only holding hands and an occasional chaste kiss or hug was considered permissible.

This concept is so foreign to Western secular culture (even in the church) where a couple will trust more in their feelings toward each other and then pray about the relationship when they are already emotionally involved. However, the very low divorce rate of Christian marriages in Uganda seemed to indicate to me that Christian marriages had a far better chance of survival there. Thus, I determined to learn all I could about success in a relationship to ensure my marriage would not only survive but would thrive!

Much as we were both convinced of God's leading in bringing us together, we had also to count the cost. Leaving father and mother and never totally fitting into the other one's culture had to be considered. There was the cost to Chris's dad in not being able to pay a dowry to my dad. Even the potential monetary cost for my having to possibly work for a Ugandan salary at some point in the future had to be discussed. I only understood the dowry issue afterwards, as I just thought it was an antiquated custom at the time. However, when a dowry is paid, the relationship between two families (not just the two individuals) is cemented. The bride becomes a member of the husband's family and leaves her own. Any children born to the couple then belong to the husband's family and will be taken care of *by them* in case of the death or ill health of the couple. If a dowry is not paid, then technically the bride has not been 'paid for' and does not belong to the husband's family in the same way. Thus, if the relationship were to break down at any point, the lady could, in fact, take the children with her and leave her husband's family—which would be a huge loss to the family.

Fortunately, since Chris's close family were themselves Christians, and I was a 'foreigner', this was not an insurmountable problem. Chris was able to reassure his father that my father was not expecting any bride price to be paid. He would probably have been more offended if it had been offered, not understanding the cultural significance! Sometimes the cost of a decision to marry cross-culturally only becomes evident over a period of time, and that is one reason why it was of crucial importance for us to know the will of God for our lives, as far as marriage was concerned. So, our time of 'dating' began. One thing Chris was concerned about was whether I could fit in with his family and accept his rural roots, as well as his urban upbringing.

In January of 1993, we got a ride on a MAF flight to Lira for the day. Chris had alerted his mother and some other family members that we were coming, so they met us at the airstrip, and we were able to visit and have lunch at the nearby Lira Hotel. This first meeting was challenging, as most of them did not speak English and I couldn't speak any Luo. However, the general impression was favourable. One person in particular, the oldest stepmum, was very excited to meet me. I didn't really understand the significance of that day, but the fact that Chris had never *dated* a lady before, yet here he was bringing me up to Lira, spoke volumes to them. Of course, his family members were expecting wedding bells from that point on! Sadly, Chris's dad couldn't make it to Lira that day, so I had to wait to meet him.

Two months later, we planned to go up to their village home, by road. I wondered if it was safe but figured that Chris wouldn't be taking me if it wasn't. I must admit I was a bit nervous. I didn't want to offend or upset Chris's family or otherwise "put my foot in it". The road wasn't the best in places. It was frequently peppered with potholes, some of axle-breaking proportions, and the 310 kilometre drive took us over five hours in a Land Rover. At this point, Chris was not able to drive, so by the time we reached our destination, I was really tired. Another thing that made this trip special (apart from my presence) was the fact that this was the first trip home for Chris since nearly dying of meningitis. As a result, folks had gathered to welcome him back to life in a very real sense! I knew this visit would be highly significant, memorable, historic, and a turning-point. What more did I need to make me even more anxious about the whole thing?

Home consisted of a circle of round, mud-brick houses with thatched roofs and a cleared space in the middle with a shady tree off to one side. Two armchairs had been prepared for us to sit on, with other chairs in a circle 'round about. They were old but clean, and I wondered about taking the best living-room type chairs and then setting them on the dirt

47

outside (very strange to my British eyes). The chairs were covered with pristine white, neatly-ironed covers and looked for all the world like two thrones! I was smiling to myself, all the while aware of the honour that this conveyed, not just to us, but to all who came to see us that day.

We all sat under the shade until gentle, but persistent, rain forced us to go inside one of the houses. A great deal of chatter and general conversation was going on, but I was not really part of it as it was almost all in Luo. I was also aware of the feeling of being an object of curiosity, which was rather uncomfortable, though there was nothing I could do about it. After about thirty minutes the rain stopped, and being a little tired of sitting, I asked where the toilet was.

"Over there," replied Chris. He pointed in a general direction with his chin (the African equivalent of nodding one's head), whilst carrying on with his previous conversation.

He seemed to have pointed towards a small, square structure of grass-panelled walls, so that's where I headed. There was no roof, just four walls that I could still peep over, two of which overlapped so that you could not see inside if you were passing by. Okay, so where was the hole in the floor? I was expecting a pit latrine, or *long drop,* as it was also called, but here there were only some broken bricks on the floor in one corner. I was puzzled. I couldn't urinate and use toilet paper (which I had in my pocket, none being available otherwise) as there was nowhere to put the used paper. I decided to do nothing and return to where I had been sitting.

Chris asked courteously, "Everything all right?"

Now here was a dilemma. Should I lie and say *yes* because it was too embarrassing to say I didn't even know how to go to the bathroom? I decided that if our relationship was to survive, it had to be based on truth, so I said an embarrassed, "No". Chris turned in surprise, wondering why I had said no. *Now* what should I say by way of explanation?

I simply said, "There was no hole". To make my embarrassment worse, he laughed and then re-directed me to the real pit latrine. I felt about an inch tall—just imagine, I didn't even know how to go to the toilet in the village! I felt like an oddball but was grateful at least that no one else knew what was going on.

Whew! I decided the latrine was a "five-star" village toilet—-it was a newly constructed, miniature mud hut. The thatch still smelled like newly cut grass, and there were no other unpleasant smells to compete with it! I duly went and made myself comfortable, but I thought to myself, "How am I going to fit here if I don't even know how to go to the toilet in the village?" Incidentally, the latrine was constructed over a dug-out anthill, and you had to step up to the top of the mound where the hole had been made. I didn't know anything about construction methods or the strength of mud in an ant hill, and just prayed that the whole thing would not collapse in on itself with me in the middle!

Sometime later in the afternoon, Chris's dad suggested Chris should take me for a walk. Great idea, I thought. I was feeling somewhat cooped up from sitting and doing little or nothing for so long. With the language barrier, I felt rather left out of things. But when I tried to talk with Chris about how the visit was going, we ended up having a serious misunderstanding. I thought he was really being insensitive and yet he was thinking something like, "If she can't fit in here, then she had better go back to Kampala tomorrow". So separately we were doing some hard thinking about the viability of our relationship, unbeknown to each other.

The rest of the visit continued, and I discovered the first grass-panelled structure I'd gone to was actually the bathing place, but also doubled as a urinal. Life was so different to anything I had known, but I managed to cope. I even began to unwind a bit when I discovered some of the relatives could actually speak English, and I could communicate with them. That first night I slept in a mud hut, mud floor and all, but it was swept spotlessly clean, and the bed and mattress were comfortable. I really slept like a baby! One of the young girls slept in the hut with me, just in case I felt lonely or anxious during the night.

Next morning, the sun was shining, and *home* didn't seem quite so strange. I got dressed and was spending time reading my Bible and praying in the little hut. I got the distinct impression; no—it was more than that. I suddenly just *knew,* without any shadow of doubt, that the confusion that we had between us the previous evening was caused, or sent to us, by a certain woman who had been present in the crowd the previous day. I could see her in my mind's eye, wearing a green dress, sitting in the corner of the house during the rain. I had not had this kind of experience before, but the Bible calls this a *word of knowledge,* and I knew this had major significance.

I shared the *word of knowledge* I'd received with Chris when he came to join me. Our breakfast was bread that we had brought the day before, along with fried liver that Chris's sister brought. He remembered the lady in the green dress but was not sure who she was. When he asked his sister, she told him the lady was the local witch doctor who lived nearby! Chris took this as confirmation that she had indeed sent a confusing demon spirit to try to break our relationship. We prayed together to bind any forces of evil that she may have unleashed. Interestingly, when she came later that day and greeted us, Chris looked her in the eye. It was as if she understood that she had been found out, and she has never stepped foot in the home again to this day.

The rest of the visit passed very cordially, and I quickly found my feet. I got to know those with whom I could speak English, and those with whom I needed an interpreter. All too soon, the few days were over, and it was time to head back to the city. The visit was a success, and Chris's folks approved of me. Within a matter of two months of relating together, I knew I was to marry Chris. He took somewhat longer to be certain, and in fact called off our relationship on more than one occasion. This did not faze me, however, as I was so sure of our future together. I just gave him his time and space and sure enough, he would come back.

I had shared about my relationship with Chris with my manager at MAF and took advantage of counselling offered by the MAF counsellor. We met on a number of occasions, and we discussed many different aspects of relationships. I know she wanted me to be sure I was not making a mistake, and I hope she went away reassured! However, we hit something of a snag. MAF policy then did not include guidelines on an unmarried missionary wanting to marry a national, so it appeared that I could not continue working for MAF and marry Chris. The answer was obvious to me—I was to marry Chris, and so I would, therefore, have to leave MAF at the end of my tour of duty in November 1993. We would have to see how God would bring us together and provide for us. Objectively and with hindsight, this was rather radical, but God gave me a supernatural gift of faith to trust Him to work things out. We prayed and applied to join a Bible College in the UK in September 1994, and we also applied to some funding agencies, as we did not have any resources for this.

Meantime, back in September 1993, we made a second visit to the village, and I was delighted to notice that I felt quite comfortable. I knew how things worked and what to expect, and I knew I was among people who were determined to like me (and I them). One really sad note about the visit was that, soon after arrival, I noticed the roof of the five-star pit latrine seemed to be smoking. On alerting everyone else, the men rushed over, but too late! The roof was well and truly on fire, and all folks could do was to watch while the thatch and roof trusses went up in flames.

How did this disaster happen? Well, periodically, to reduce the flies in a pit latrine, smoke is used to kill them or chase them away. One of the young boys was given the task of getting a bundle of smouldering grass stalks and dropping them down into the hole. However, he seemed a novice at the task. When he did it, the bundle came loose and some of the stalks stuck onto the sides of the hole instead of dropping down. The hot gases rising from the latrine were enough to ignite the smouldering grass, and the rest was history.

What a shame! However, we had a bigger dilemma now—no pit latrine. Since it is a major task to construct a new latrine, the men had to improvise and make the existing one useable, even if it had no roof. So, they made a grass-panel screen in front of the door space (there was no actual door) so no one could see in as you went in. First problem solved. Second problem was that of the ant hill in the middle. Remember? You had to step up on to the top of it to use the toilet. Now, because the roof was no longer there, I had to bend over as I stepped up so that I couldn't be seen over the top of the wall! It sure required a bit of gymnastics to do the necessaries, but I managed. Again, the visit proved a success.

CHAPTER 9

The MAF Story Continued

T ime passed, and I had to return to the UK for four months of home assignment (or furlough) before my employment with, and support from, MAF would end. Being apart from Chris was hard, and we both gave a lot of business to the postal service in our long, newsy and romantic letters going back and forth! Meantime, we waited for the Bible college application to be processed.

Back in Scotland, it was so easy to get back into the swing of things. I enjoyed my church life and activities and also went to other churches and groups, talking about the work of MAF and encouraging people to support the work. Looking back, I realised it was so good to get back to a way of life that was so totally familiar and comfortable. There was no need to wonder whether I was misreading circumstances or what someone was saying.

Just before Christmas, I saw a temporary job advertised with my former employer, the Highland Regional Council (HRC). It was a few pay grades below what I had previously been employed at, but since it was related to some of my previous work, I thought I might have a chance of succeeding with an application. The job was for sixteen weeks, commencing in March 1994 and involved administration of local council elections, which were due to be held. *Great timing*, I thought. It would provide an income until the summer. I prayed and sent in the application. Out of over 200 applicants, somehow, I found favour and was offered the contract in January 1994, to start working in March. After consulting with Chris, I accepted. In the meanwhile, as Chris's application was being considered by the Bible college, he was asked to do a book review, which he duly did and sent it to them.

We had a visiting preacher at our church one Sunday. Although I can't remember his name or the subject of his sermon, there was one thing that stuck in my mind. He said, "If you feel you haven't heard from God for some time, it could be that you have made a wrong decision in your life. So, look back and review any decisions you might have made around the time you feel God last spoke to you. It could be that it was a wrong decision".

I identified with that, as I felt that I hadn't heard from God directly for some time. In fact, when I analysed things, it was since we decided to apply to the Bible college. I prayed and asked God to make His will plain for my life and for Chris. Not many days later, I got a letter from Chris saying the Bible college application had been turned down. He was considered too *Pentecostal* to fit into the interdenominational college! I should have been disappointed, since this was to have been the means to bring us back together, but in view of the sermon the previous Sunday, instead I rejoiced. For me, this would bring us back into God's will for our lives, and He would then be the One to bring us together, not any plan of our own. I decided to ring Chris, despite the cost, to tell him that I felt this was a good thing. He was much relieved at my reaction, since with hindsight, he too, had not had total peace with the application. We rejoiced together and agreed to continue to pray and ask God to open a way for us and that He would order our lives so that we would be able to get married.

I started my new job in March and enjoyed the challenge. I had been working for about two weeks when I got an unexpected phone call from MAF. The personnel officer wanted to know whether I could still be available to work in Uganda since they had failed to find a replacement for me. I said I would be available in July but still felt it was God's will for me to marry Chris. I think maybe he was hoping that I had forgotten about Chris or the marriage plans.

He said, 'Oh, I see. Well, I'll have to get back to you'.

I wrote and told Chris but didn't get my hopes up. However, the personnel officer did call back and offered me a temporary contract for six months while they continued to look for my replacement. Both Chris and I felt that if this was God's way of taking me back to Uganda, then we would accept. I agreed to a return date of July 1994, some four weeks after finishing the HRC contract. MAF undertook to make good my financial support shortfall, since I would not have time to do any significant support raising.

Naturally, I had shared all of this with my church leadership and, of course, they wanted an opportunity to meet Chris. The wise advice I had been given was that Chris should see me in my home culture before we made any decision to marry. My family also wanted to meet Chris; however, I couldn't see how a visit to the UK would be at all possible. Neither of us had any money to pay for his air ticket. God had a plan, though. Out of the blue, one of the older women in the church, Auntie Grace, offered to lend Chris the money for his air ticket and a little spending money. She said he could pay her back whenever he had the money. This was most unusual, even unheard of. Chris was able to make plans to come to the UK in June and spend a month there with me before we returned to Uganda together to plan our wedding.

Where we should get married was another cultural dilemma. In British culture, the couple marries at the bride's church. In Uganda, the couple marries at the groom's church, and ours was all the more important since Chris was a pastor in KPC. So, I had to tell my family and church that we would not be able to get married in Scotland but in Uganda instead.

I dutifully finished my HRC contract and went down to London to meet Chris. He had arrived some days earlier and was visiting with some of his relatives who live in London. We spent the weekend, meeting up with them, and then headed on to Inverness. Chris had something of a strange feeling on the plane when he realised that he was the only black person on board! 'Guess how I feel in Uganda sometimes?' was my reply.

Meeting with my parents was the first hurdle. We travelled to stay with them for a week, and I wondered how to broach the subject of our impending marriage with them. My dad instead surprised me a couple of days into the visit, by asking, *'So, what are your plans for the future then?'* They loved Chris and thought very highly of him. My dad even went as far as calling him *son*! You can imagine I was thrilled that they really liked him and had given us the green light for our wedding.

Similarly, meeting with my church leaders and Christian family went well, as did meeting up with my brothers and their families and other relatives in England. All approved of Chris and liked his character and personality, and gave their approval to our wedding plans. I knew my elderly parents would not make it to the wedding, and I wasn't sure whether my brothers would make it, either, as Uganda was still in the 'back of beyond' in most people's thinking.

We arrived back in Uganda together in July 1994 and, as I started back at work with MAF, we started our wedding preparations.

CHAPTER 10

The Cross-Cultural Wedding Experience

I had not known that in Christian circles in Uganda, the friends of the intending couple were the ones who, in fact, organised their wedding! Chris's friends particularly formed a committee, which was responsible for drawing up a budget for the wedding (in consultation with us, of course). They then raised all the funds to cover the cost of the wedding day. They also made sure that things happened as they should on the big day. Their duties covered everything from getting the bride and groom to the hairdresser first thing in the morning to ensuring the best man, groomsmen, bridesmaids, and matron (or maid) of honour all got ready in time to making sure the bride and groom were not late, either! All I had to do was have my dress and my honeymoon suitcase ready before the big day.

As it turned out, none of my family was able to attend the wedding, but God graced our marriage celebration. On 15 October 1994, we were pronounced 'husband and wife'. The church was jam-packed, and the sense of celebration and jubilation was exhilarating. I had decided that I was not going to let anything spoil my special day. Being a born organiser, it was difficult for me to leave everything to others to organise, but I had no choice, so I just sat back and determined to relax and enjoy myself. As it happened, I had no need to be concerned, as all went according to plan.

The weather was sunny, but not too hot; we all looked very beautiful and handsome. Gorgeous flowers and ribbons decorated the church. The wedding service was joyful and honouring to God. The photography session took place in the gardens of the Sheraton Hotel amidst lovely flowers and shrubs, and the reception was fun! I truly felt like the Queen of the Day.

A wedding reception in Uganda is quite different. Since so many individuals contribute to paying for the wedding through the fund-raising efforts of the organising committee, thus making it a success, everyone is automatically invited to the reception. At the time we were married, it was the norm for the guests to be served soft drinks or soda, with perhaps a cake and a samosa or a piece of fried meat. Our guests had all that and more to spare.

We were entertained by several youth bands who had all wanted the privilege of singing at their pastor's wedding. The wedding cake was unusual, a real work of art. It had many tiers and was made up into the shape of a church. It is the tradition that after the refreshments have been served and all the speeches have been made, the bride and groom go out to change into the clothes they will wear as they leave the reception. At that point, the guests are led in a time of singing of lively and joyful praise songs. Our guests were so enthusiastic and happy that two people had to hold the wedding cake table steady. Guests danced around it at the front of the room, just below the stage, where the high table was situated.

Chris and I had had white lace, Nigerian-style changing clothes made, and we looked very regal as we marched back in to the reception. It was a shame we had to cut the cake; it looked so lovely! However, all good things must come to an end, and so did the reception. We made our *thank you* speech to the guests and left for the final event of the day. If the wedding was exciting, so was the after-party. This was a more informal get-together for all the family and close friends who had worked so hard during the day. A veritable feast had been prepared as our *thank you* to them. Everyone was so happy for us, and at last we could relax and have fun in the pleasant cool of the evening. Our best man finally took us to our hotel at 9.30 p.m. What a fabulous day!

I have gone into some detail about our courtship days— the ups and downs, times that were funny and then serious, encouraging and disappointing. However, at the end of the day, we can truly say that God was directing the whole process, and we can say without any shadow of doubt that He was the One who made our marriage possible. With hindsight, I believe that there is a *checklist* with three main objectives for a lasting relationship. Firstly, knowing that it is God who has brought you together. Secondly, establishing a genuine friendship, based on common interests and hobbies. Thirdly, having shared values about the deep concerns of life—spiritual beliefs, character, principles of integrity, and visions and dreams for life together.

We have found that pre-marriage preparation is important in helping a newly married couple to adjust to life together, and ours was detailed and extensive. The more time a couple spends in preparation for marriage, the easier the adjustment will be. Discussing topics such as finances, in-laws, children, family devotional time, handling conflict, and so on will bring to the surface any major differences that can be ironed out in advance. Lifelong commitment is a must for any successful, lasting relationship. The Bible teaches that marriage is a covenant, not a contract that can be broken at any time. Knowing we were both in for the long haul and that we committed ourselves to sorting out *any problem* as quickly as possible, and *no matter the cost* gave us both a sense of security. For us, divorce is not an option. Instead we *choose* to love each other every day, whether we feel like it or not!

CHAPTER 11

The Cross-Cultural
Honeymoon Experience

I think one vital ingredient in any serious relationship is a sense of humour. Ours was tested on our wedding night! We had planned to spend our wedding night in one of the hotels in Kampala before heading off for our honeymoon on Sunday. I had been to the hotel twice to make sure the booking was made and confirmed, and we had even paid for the room in advance just the day before. Applying the principle that *if anything can go wrong, it will*, I had three times specified that this was our wedding night, and that we wanted a double bed—one large bed, not two small ones. I had painstakingly explained this to the man at the hotel reception.

Chris's best man dropped us at the hotel in the evening. Imagine our surprise, disbelief, dismay even, when we were taken to a room with twin beds at 9.30 p.m. on the evening of our wedding! I was *not* prepared to accept such incompetence. I told the bellboy we had booked a double room, one with only one bed, as this was our wedding night. He came back after twenty minutes, saying that all the double rooms were taken.

'Why were we not told that *last night* when we came to pay for the room?' I asked him.

He gave us a lame excuse that everyone who was staying in the double rooms last night had decided to stay on. So, there was no double room available now. And he expected us to believe that? I told him to find us a double room, or we wanted our money back and we would go elsewhere. Again, he left—but this time came back after five minutes.

'*Follow me*', he said, then promptly took us to a double room.

Now why tell a lie and say *there is no room available* when, in fact, there was? Well, we just gave thanks to God. Some things you don't get an answer to. I'm not sure what kind of impression this stubborn, insistent woman made on Chris, but he did not comment at the time. He was, no doubt just as delighted as I to have a bed available, rather than the unenviable task of finding another in Kampala at that time of night!

We had a wonderful honeymoon, but again, things didn't really go too smoothly. The air ticket that the office messenger had bought for me from Entebbe to Nairobi had the wrong initial in my name. So, we had to use some of our precious dollars of spending money at the airport to buy me another ticket. When we got to Jomo Kenyatta airport in Nairobi, there was a MAF family who was supposed to meet us with our onward air tickets to Mombasa. They were *not waiting for us* at the arrivals hall and, after looking 'round the airport and not finding them anywhere, we decided all we could do was to pray and wait and not get anxious.

Fortunately, God answers prayer, and we bumped in to them an hour or so later. What a relief! We flew to Mombasa a little later and then caught a taxi to go to our hotel. We had booked it through a mission agency in Nairobi in order to get a good price. Again, I had told them we wanted a double room, as it was our honeymoon. You know, it is a bit embarrassing having to belabour the point about wanting one bed to sleep in for our honeymoon; it was definitely worth the extra effort! We decided if we didn't stick our necks out, then we would end up putting up with something we didn't really want.

Imagine when we got to the hotel, we were shown into—you guessed it—a twin-bedded room! Once again, I had to explain, but this time we were shown immediately into a double room with lots of apologies from the manager on duty.

We had a great holiday, including beautiful sunshine, clean, white coral, sandy beaches, good food, a quiet location, and a cooling breeze blowing in from the Indian Ocean. Idyllic is the word. In fact, Mombasa is the best-known holiday destination in East Africa. The hotel service was excellent, and the climate was fabulous without being oppressively hot. However, all too soon, we had to head back home.

For our return journey to Nairobi, we had decided to take a luxury minibus but imagine our disbelief when we saw a policeman impounding the very vehicle we were supposed to travel in—and right in front of our noses. To this day we don't know why that happened, but we had to argue with the company to get seats on the regular bus that was just about to leave. Then, more arguing for a cash refund, since the bus was a cheaper means of travel. It was a hot, dusty, crowded, and bumpy means of travel, but I kept reminding myself it was all part of the adventure.

To get back to Uganda from Kenya, we had booked seats on the MAF plane from Wilson Airport to Entebbe. However, once again we had a mix-up, as there was no MAF flight on that day! Somehow, we managed to be squeezed on an AIM flight instead, and we made it home. Unfortunately, our suitcase got ripped in the aircraft, so the pilot ended up giving us a refund of the equivalent of one fare, and we got back to Uganda at half price. It was not quite how we had planned it, but we were back and ready to set up home as husband and wife with our very own double bed.

Problems and challenges come in life—that is guaranteed! We found that it is *how we react* to them that matters. We learned to smile, not lose any sleep, solve the problem, and move on.

CHAPTER 12

The Cross-Cultural Extended Family Experience

A rriving back home was when we really had to learn to adjust to living together. Prior to our marriage, Chris had between three and five family members staying with him at various times. Now that we were husband and wife, he had the wisdom to find them all alternative places to live. So, we came to our new home, just the two of us, and a house-girl that we employed to look after the place and cook, wash and iron for us, since we were both working full-time. Chris's reasoning was that I should establish the house to run the way I wanted so that when his relatives came to visit or stay, they would have to fit into our household routine. Smart thinking, and thanks to Chris's thoughtfulness, that is, in fact, what happened. Indeed, coming from my relatively small family, the number of Chris's relatives was rather overwhelming. So, in this way I was able to get to know them gradually, and things worked out very well.

How to manage each other's family members can often be a source of conflict between young marrieds, so I was very grateful for the wise and sensitive way Chris managed his family. His actions really confirmed that I was more important to him than even his family members.

Another major challenge was time-keeping. I am an early bird. I like to get up early, set about my routine for the day, and then go to bed fairly early, too. Chris is a night owl, preferring to go to bed late and get up in a relaxed way in the morning. How to do two opposites like that manage to adjust? Well, you have to, if you want to have a happy time together. I had to relax my need for a fixed routine and learn to sometimes go to bed later than I would ordinarily choose. He had to adjust to the fact that I would be getting up early. We both had to compromise our preferences at times to accommodate one another's needs.

In terms of keeping time for events or occasions, we had to strike a deal. If the event or occasion was one that had been organised by Ugandans, then Chris would determine the time that we would leave home to reach the venue. If the event was organised by expatriates, then I would be the one setting the timetable. We had to do this, as most Ugandan functions did not happen on time, and if you came at the stipulated time, you could end up waiting for two or even three frustrating hours till things actually began. Chris had to allow me to set the pace on some occasions where I knew people would be keeping to a scheduled time. The one thing we were and are never late for is church on Sundays, as the services always start on time!

Mealtimes, specifically the timing of our evening meal was somewhat erratic to begin with, depending on whether there was a meeting at church, or at work, that either Chris or I was involved in. Previously, Chris had been used to eating whenever supper was ready (even as late as 11 p.m.), not necessarily having supper ready at a particular time. That was usually the custom in Uganda, since many folks would buy their supper on the way home from work and then have to start cooking it. With few people being able to afford a refrigerator, food was bought fresh and consumed that same day.

Since we were blessed to have a fridge, we could organise our lives a little more. To start with, I hated eating late and going to bed with a full stomach. On the other hand, Chris was used to going to sleep feeling pleasantly full and satisfied. Definitely a discussion and some flexibility were in order, and a gradual change has seen us aiming to have supper between 6 p.m. and 7 p.m. We also discovered the mealtime could change, depending on our circumstances and lifestyle at the time, so each couple or family needs to work out what is most convenient or possible for them.

Money is another major area that often causes conflict between couples, and it was good that we talked about financial matters in our pre-marriage preparation, so that this area did not take us by surprise. At the time we married, I was earning quite a bit more than Chris. This could have been hard for him to accept, and so I took great pains to reassure him that all we earned, from whatever source, was *ours*—not mine or his. I had a bank account in the UK, and Chris had an account in Uganda. When we got married, we changed both of the accounts to joint accounts, with either of us authorised to make any transactions on them. Of course, what happened was that we both discussed any transactions we felt were needed to make on either of the accounts.

In addition, we drew up a family budget, so we would know, month by month, how we would cover our financial commitments and from what source the money would be funded. Needs are always more than your income, especially in Africa, so if we had funds in our account that we had identified as designated funds, then we had no problem with refusing non-budgeted financial requests. This at least took some pressure off our finances.

The early years of our marriage were challenging at times. Imagine two strong personalities suddenly sharing all aspects of their lives, when we were both a little older and rather set in our ways (Chris was almost thirty-three, and I was thirty-six)—a recipe for differences of opinion, for sure. It was good to have one year by ourselves with no family members staying at our home, so that a few of the rough edges could be smoothed over, and our arguments were not overheard by anyone else.

We had to keep reminding each other that we did not intentionally mean to hurt each other, and then pray for the

Lord to change one's own attitude or heart over an issue. Of course, the way God works in my marriage when I pray is to change *me*, not my spouse. The sooner I grasped that principle, the better it was for both of us. It can be a temptation to continually ask God to change *him* instead of *me*.

We also had to decide, as a family, which of the many needy children in the family that we could sponsor or pay school fees for. This is an issue for many African families but is something of a foreign concept if one spouse is used to education that is free of charge. I could see the need and so freely agreed to assist in sending several of the many nieces and nephews to school, especially those who were either orphans or had only a mother living. We continued with assistance right through tertiary education.

I discovered our commitment to those children did not, however, stop at paying fees, After a couple of years, they came to spend holidays in our home. They became 'our' children—imagine becoming a mother of teenagers before having babies! It wasn't that easy for me, having what felt like a houseful and trying to bridge the cultural and age gaps. Somehow, we all survived! Perhaps we even thrived as we had to grow through all the challenges for our family life to be enjoyable. God had another purpose with all of the nurturing of these children through to adulthood, as we shall later see.

CHAPTER 13

The Cross-Cultural Clashes

After the early years of adjustment, life and ministry settled into something of a routine. As we learned to communicate more effectively, we understood each other better. Home was a peaceful place, full of fun. We still had our challenges to work through, but these changed over time. Once we had the small issues sorted out, fewer, but seemingly more important, ones would surface. This is, however, common in all marriages, so this part of our adjustment was right on target.

Since childhood, my dad had taught me how to tackle any and all jobs around the house—a good thing, since I lived on my own before coming out to Uganda. Changing a light bulb, fixing a plug on an appliance, mowing the lawn, and keeping the garden neat and tidy, and minor repairs here and there were things I used to do as a matter of routine. I was very independent in this respect. However, I soon discovered in my marriage that these jobs or repairs were considered a man's tasks, and by doing them, I was undermining Chris's role in the family. Since he was not the most prompt of guys in undertaking these tasks, I had to choose. I could either do the job and undermine my husband or grin and bear the frustration of not having something fixed in good time. I learned to grin and keep quiet instead.

I began to understand that God had designed men and women to have different roles within a marriage relationship (not the same, as I had thought at first). It dawned on me that men and women were made differently in order to complement each other's strengths and weaknesses. For a marriage to work smoothly, it made sense that there should be only one with the responsibility to lead the family—the trousers weren't made for us both to wear! Once I realised these foundational truths, life within our marriage became much more peaceful as we both began to pull together in the same direction, as it were.

God also had to deal with my independent streak. Imagine living with someone who you perceive doesn't need you! It was not very uplifting for my husband, so I had to learn to *not* do things sometimes, but to allow Chris to do them instead. I had to learn to demonstrate to Chris that I needed him in my life. The Bible tells a man to *love* his wife but tells the woman to *respect* her husband (Ephesians 6). These two commands reflect the need of a woman to *receive* love and affirmation from her husband and the need of a man to be *given* honour and respect by his wife. The man is instructed first; in other words, as the man showers love on his wife, she will automatically show him respect and honour.

The commands do not appear the other way around, which is interesting in the traditional African context. Many men still have the traditional view that the wife is subservient, and the husband can virtually order her to show respect to him at all times. Sadly, such relationships have missed the vitally important principle that so long as he showers love on her, she will normally automatically respond with honour and respect. Thankfully Chris was not traditional in his approach to our marriage. Willingness on both our parts to learn, change, and grow has contributed to success in our marriage thus far.

For you, these truths might be obvious, but for me, they were more like a revelation. They did help me to get a better, or rather biblical, perspective on my relationship with Chris and within our marriage. I stopped expecting Chris to do certain things as I thought he should do them to help me. I also stopped doing the things which undermined or disrespected him. And I stopped getting frustrated whilst waiting for a job to get done (or I asked someone else to do it).

To better understand myself, my husband and marriage in general, I decided to invest in good books on the subject. God could, therefore, challenge me in the areas of my life that needed to be changed, and by His grace, I slowly made progress. I had realised from the outset that I could never change anything about Chris. If he had a habit or characteristic I didn't like, then I learned to raise the issue with him quietly and calmly *once*. After that, if there was no change in him, then it was up to me to handle my own reaction to the issue, whatever it was. Minor issues are not worth losing either sleep or peace over!

Gradually our home has become a blend of our two birth cultures but with overriding Christian principles guiding all aspects of our lives. Naturally, our home has more of a Ugandan flavour since the overwhelming majority of our household is Ugandan. However, it is obvious that my culture has influenced how we live our lives as well as the customs and traditions that we have established for ourselves. *Where* you decide to set up your home very definitely influences the culture that you establish in your home. However, every relationship is a blend of the habits and customs of the two individuals and so, in a sense, each marriage must establish its own culture. We have done this, and our culture is a blend of both our backgrounds and life experiences.

However, all this assumed stability can change remarkably quickly. For example, when we visited the UK in 1996 for a period of three months, I instantly reverted back to my British culture, that is, according to Chris. I was not even aware of any change! This was bewildering to him, and he was left wondering what had happened to his wife. When he had no other relatives nearby, you can imagine how alone this made him feel. Similarly, although to a much lesser extent, when we visit Chris's mother at our village 'home', Chris reverts to the culture he grew up in, and naturally all conversation is in his mother tongue, leaving me to feel left out or alone.

The one who is on his or her home turf is not aware that they have changed their patterns of behaviour. They are so happy being back to their roots that they can become particularly insensitive to the isolation being felt by their spouse. So, a word of caution to those married or intending to marry cross-culturally: be extra sensitive to each other's needs when you move to a different country or region. We choose to see such instances not as problems but as areas for personal growth and for growth within our marriage. Coming from two very different cultures can bring significant challenges, but also the inherent differences bring additional richness and blessings. It all depends on how you look at things.

CHAPTER 14

The Miraculous Provision

O ver time, I have realised that the *home* is very important to a woman. Perhaps it's the God-ordained mothering/nesting instinct that is within us, or perhaps it is tied to our need for our family, to belong somewhere. In Uganda, I have had several homes, but the feature of each one was that it would be a place where I could be safe and secure. The one common factor was the burglar proofing and a night guard. In common with housing in many countries, these are necessary deterrents in Uganda to avoid the would-be thief. However, burglar-proofing can also be a potential deathtrap, in that there is no way to get *out* of a window in the case of fire. In fact, MAF used to make it a part of any house-rental agreement that they could modify one window, usually toward the back of the house, to make it so that the burglar-proofing bars could open. It was then kept padlocked from the inside. Fortunately, I have not as yet known of a major house fire amongst our circle of acquaintance.

Guards are a very interesting group of people. Few do the work because they are interested in security or law and order. For many, they work during the night and have another job during part of the day. So, when do they get a chance to sleep? You guessed it! During the night of course. It was not uncommon to wake in the night and hear the gentle snores of the night guard. It made me realise that my security was not in the frailty of a human being or in bars on the windows (though these have their part to play) but in the angels I believe the good Lord deploys around my house every night. This, however, took me time to realise.

When I stopped working with MAF, we had to move to another house, and we could not—at that point—afford to have a night guard. So, while we were looking for a place to stay, I remember asking God for a place where I would feel safe and secure. Some close friends of ours asked us if we would like to rent their old house at a very reasonable rent. We naturally said *yes*. We had been living there for some weeks when I remembered what I had told God that I needed to feel secure. I think He has quite a sense of humour as the house we had moved to had very high walls all around, topped with jagged pieces of broken glass—a great deterrent to any would-be thief!

Some four years later, we moved into a house we were able to construct. Interestingly, the garden is open to Lake Victoria at the bottom, and we still have no night guard. I feel totally at peace and secure now, knowing my security and safety is in God's hands. Our house, rather our *home*, is a place of rest and peace, a place where you can forget about the stresses and busyness of life and recharge your batteries, so to speak. At the time we'd started to think about building our own place, we had very little money. Chris had seen half an acre of land beside the lake, but we never thought we would be able to buy it, let alone build.

However, God spoke to Chris and asked him, 'Is this the place you would call home?' Of course, the answer was *yes*, and God instructed him, '*Build my church and I will build your home*'. We were not sure at that point what that exactly meant but took note of the words. Amazingly, the funds to purchase the land came together in the ensuing two weeks, and by the time negotiations with the seller were concluded and the contract ready for signing, the cash was ready! We were truly amazed.

When it came to drawing-up building plans and starting construction, the test came. We had an urgent fundraising campaign at church to buy a car park adjacent to the church. Chris and I had a small amount of cash in the bank with which to start building the house. Then we remembered what God had told us about building *His house*, and we knew that we had to give the little we had saved towards the fund to buy the church car park. Without hesitation, we did so.

We were able to start building the house through a small, unsecured loan from our bank in Scotland and an advance of house rent from church. Thus, began the series of miracles that ended up in our being able to move into our partly finished house just one year later! Some individuals gave us unexpected gifts, and we would discover that what they gave was just what we needed to finish the roof or the ceiling or the windows or whatever it was that we had just calculated the cost to complete. It was as if God took the little we had and multiplied it, just as Jesus had performed the miracle of multiplying the five loaves and two fish to feed five thousand men, plus the women and children, two thousand years ago! When we took a step of faith, the resources came to meet the need. God indeed did supply what we needed to build our house, as He had promised us. After moving in, God continued to supply until we were able to complete it all before we brought our children home!

Of course, right from the outset, we wanted our home to be used to bless others. The garden, for example, is used to hold meetings of various types from time to time, as well as wedding receptions, and we love to have visitors over to stay. I have been reminded many times over the years of the words of Jesus in Mark's Gospel, chapter 10, verses 29–30:

> No-one who has left home or brothers or sisters
> or mother or father or children or fields for me
> and the gospel will fail to receive a hundred
> times as much in this present age (homes,

brothers, sisters, mothers, children and fields –
and with them persecutions) and in the age to
come, eternal life.

God has given me very many relatives through my marriage to Chris, and very many spiritual children and siblings as
I do His work in Uganda. Not only that, but of the things I had
to give up, as it were, in coming to Uganda, I have never been
without as I serve Him. I drive a better car, I live in a far more
beautiful home, and I have a wonderful husband and children.
I can honestly say that though it was (and is) hard to leave my
own family back in the UK, God has fulfilled His promises to me.

CHAPTER 15

Cross-Cultural Concepts

D iversity was very quickly demonstrated in our household in a tangible way. Having an early morning cup of tea was a tradition for me, so when we got married, I made some for Chris, too. I made sure the water was boiling well, warmed up the teapot, made the tea, and left it under the tea cosy to brew. I added a little cold milk to the cups and poured the tea. Lovely? Wrong! I forgot that Chris's expectation of a good cup of tea was quite different. In Uganda, milk (sometimes diluted with a little water) is brought to a boil in a saucepan, at which point loose tea leaves are added to the boiling milk and allowed to boil and infuse for a few minutes. Sugar is then added—-preferably generously—and the tea is strained into the cup for serving. Sometimes a special blend of sweet spices is added to flavour the tea. Now which is the right way to make tea? Of course, both.

Instead of knowing only one way to make tea, I now knew two. And I learned the lesson of allowing differences to bring diversity, not division. Although this is a somewhat trivial example, the principle I learned through it is widely applicable.

Another early difference that emerged had to do with communication. In most Ugandan cultures, it is better to tell someone a lie or avoid the truth, rather than tell someone something they would not want to hear. If you are invited to a function, for example, and you already have two commitments at that particular time, you should rather say, 'Yes, I'm a bit busy, but I'll try my best', rather than be straight and explain you can't make it. This caused some initial embarrassment to Chris, as I did not understand the need for diplomacy or respect in letting someone down gently. Over time, he has learned to be more direct, and I have learned to be direct but in a diplomatic or sensitive way. This quickly became part of our personal growth and development.

How about something as simple as caring for the pet dog? In Uganda, a dog is kept outside and is fed scraps or leftovers of food that no one else wants. You would not buy special or tinned food for the dog. If you were to buy food, it would be the cheapest and poorest quality maize meal to cook with cheap small dried fish.

I had been in the habit of buying what I thought was cheap meat to feed my Alsatian guard dogs till I met Chris and realised that he only occasionally bought meat for his family (his income was rather low at the time). I therefore changed the dog's diet to the small fish, but one dog wasn't impressed at all. He would look disdainfully down his long nose when his evening meal was put before him. He'd lost quite a lot of weight before he finally and begrudgingly gave in and started eating the fish/maize flour food! With time, he got used to it. I used to let him wander in the house during the day, since the door was always open. He wasn't averse to climbing up onto the settee to have his afternoon nap! I didn't approve of this, but Chris thought I was crazy to allow the dog inside like a human being! As for a pet being regarded as a part of the family, well, that's a foolish Western concept. Hmm.

Where do you spend the greatest part of your time at home or your leisure time, I wonder? Life in Uganda, outside of the city, is largely lived outdoors. People only come inside when it is cold, wet or dark. In the UK, however, we live life indoors and only go outside when it's nice and warm and sunny, or when we have to work in the garden. Completely opposite concepts that it took me a while to figure out.

Chris and I do, however, spend quite a bit of time inside in the cool of the living room, and only go out to sit in the shade with a nice breeze. I rarely sunbathe in Uganda, and yet in the UK, I couldn't wait for spring and summer to come in order to sit outside to get a bit of colour on my skin! In fact, I discovered when you live and work in the heat, the last thing you want to do when you get home, or when you have some time off is to sit in the hot sun. Just as well, considering the strength of the sun's rays near the equator, I guess.

Generally, in Uganda, age is respected and even venerated. An integral part of all the tribal cultures is showing respect to those older than you. Kneeling, when greeting someone of a generation older than you, is a very common gesture of respect. Once I understood that this was a mark of respect, I too had no problem with kneeling to greet Chris's dad and mum, much to the delight of the family. Sure, it felt a bit odd the first time or two, but I soon got used to it. I think this honour of the elderly is very healthy (as well as biblical) in any culture, and I found it very refreshing. However, that simple act of respect, when translated into a Western culture, could be seen as subservience or an extreme kind of submission or even repression.

I soon found out that my *British* English wasn't necessarily understood here in Uganda, even though English is the official national language. I had to learn that language is not static but grows and evolves with time. Thus, the English spoken since Uganda received her independence from Britain in 1962 has changed noticeably. Also, since English is, in fact, a second language to 99 per cent of the population, many expressions in Ugandan English are transliterated from indigenous languages, giving rise to a new set of interesting expressions and idioms.

When Chris told me one time to 'put milk on fire', I had to think twice and realise that he meant for me to heat up some milk on the cooker. Many times, if I had been away for a week, people would greet me at church and say, 'You're lost'! The first time or two, I had to assure them I was not lost and that

I knew where I was. Then the penny dropped, and I realised they were in fact saying, 'I haven't seen you for a while'. At least then I knew how to respond to their greeting. One of my nieces told me one day that she was going to 'give a visitor a push'. *Push her where?* I wondered. *Ah, it means as she is leaving, I'm going to walk up the road a little way with her.* Interesting!

We all know laughter is the best medicine, but what causes you to laugh? Different things are funny to different people, I discovered. Some things make Chris and I both laugh, but some things that Chris laughs at, I don't find funny at all. I can be chuckling away to myself, and when I explain to Chris, he looks blankly at me. Well, we just accept that our humour is different, and we laugh at the same time at the same thing only sometimes!

How about grey hair? What about it, you may ask? Well, generally Caucasians will get grey hair far earlier than Africans, and indeed Africans seem to get fewer wrinkles around the eyes, too. So, at the age of 40, a Caucasian lady may end up looking much older than her African husband! My solution to that is, of course, to dye my hair, and pray that Chris soon starts to get a few grey hairs of his own to even the equation. Interestingly, he would be very happy about having some grey hair as it would make him more respected and distinguished. In fact, he cherishes the one that appears in the middle of his beard, but it keeps falling out!

One time, we had just come back from a relaxing holiday, and I looked nice and tanned, with a few extra pounds on me, showing that I had been pampered. When I went into the office, the cleaning lady exclaimed, 'Oh, you look so nice'! Having been in Africa for a number of years by then, I knew she meant, 'Oh, haven't you put on weight?' I had to smile and thank her but really wasn't too pleased to be reminded that I looked obviously fatter. In Africa, when a lady puts on weight, especially when she is married, it means that her husband is taking good care of her and feeding her well. So, in this case, she concluded I had had a good time eating and being cared for whilst on holiday! Another reason ladies (and men for that matter) in Uganda do not wish to look thin is that the nickname for HIV/AIDS here is 'slim' because sufferers lose weight and end up being very thin. Thus, Ugandans would much rather look 'well-rounded'.

I discovered that Chris's family didn't really have a culture of remembering or celebrating birthdays or anniversaries, whereas in my family, we had always done so. It was considered important to acknowledge such occasions. Since it meant so much to me, I had to explain these celebrations to Chris, and he decided to adopt that custom for our family, as much for my sake as anything else. Of course, it becomes even more important when children come onto the scene, as a special birthday celebration means so much to them. I think he rather likes celebrating birthdays now, as he knows I will bake a special birthday cake!

Another thing that is rare in Ugandan cultures is for a husband to say 'I love you' to his wife. Rather, he demonstrates love by providing the home, food and other basic necessities for her. Chris didn't really subscribe to that view and has been free to express how he feels to me. We've also had quite an influence on other couples in this area as we counsel them. It is interesting to see how the flower of romance flourishes when it's watered in the right way! This issue prompted us to discuss how to express our love and appreciation to each other. I prefer tangible ways, such as flowers now and again, or a card, e-mail or note, but I had to explain that to Chris. I couldn't just expect him to know this, much as such gifts are supposed to be unprompted! Mind you, I was perplexed one day when he came home with a bag of green apples. I knew they were imported from South Africa and VERY expensive. He must have seen my puzzled expression, so he explained that flowers quickly die off, but at least you can eat apples and get benefit from them. Interesting...... but I STILL prefer flowers. Some things you just can't explain logically.

One time when he had to go away, I wrote about ten small notes of appreciation and hid them in Chris's suitcase—-in his toilet bag, his clothes, in his Bible, and even in his underwear. He had great fun finding these little surprises and was constantly reminded of my love for him. He is good at remembering to buy flowers when I least expect them, and they are all the more appreciated for that. Much as it takes some of the delight away when you have to explain what you'd like to receive, it is better to do just that because your spouse can't get inside your head to read your thoughts or to know what makes you tick, unless you tell him/her. It really pays in the long run.

CHAPTER 16

Cross Cultural Adoption

There is an African proverb, 'It takes a village to raise a child'. In times gone by, that was so true; African life was *lived communally*. Relationships with people matter more than anything else. Children were—and still are—cared for by each and every member of a family, clan and village.

Girl children are valued because, as they become of marriageable age, the successful suitor will need to bring cows and other valuable items to his bride-to-be's family as the dowry for the girl. She, therefore, marries into her husband's family and leaves her family home, having brought wealth to the family in the process. Girls are brought up to be hard-working and knowledgeable so that they will bring credit to their parents. Boy children, on the other hand, are valued because they will stay at home and provide the continuity the family needs. They will have to pay a dowry in order to bring their brides into the family and will ensure the family continues to grow as they have children of their own. Boys are brought up to be responsible and are not afraid of the hard work of digging in the garden.

A young bride who doesn't get pregnant soon after marriage is of concern to the family elders. It is automatically assumed that the problem lies with the woman, and those who do not hold to Christian values will, even today, take a second wife in order to get children. Chris and I decided to wait a year after our marriage before trying for a child. I fell pregnant shortly thereafter, but sadly lost the little embryonic baby soon after. I was so thankful that I was not condemned by anyone in the family for the fact that no baby was forthcoming. I have to say, that I think we left it too late to start thinking of family as I later discovered a woman's fertility reduces drastically after the age of thirty-five.

A few years went by, and we considered going for fertility treatment but in the end did not. We considered adoption, but after we had discussed the idea, I thought Chris was not in favour. (It turned out years later, that he thought it was *me* who was not in favour of the idea. It just shows how misunderstandings can happen so easily, even over such an important issue.) We had been prayed for by a number of God's people over the years, but no miracle came for us. There were times when we were full of faith and expected a baby to come any time, and there were other times when we despaired. But we never lost faith in the Lord, knowing He would fill the yearning in our hearts, realising that He knows what is best for us.

After nine years of marriage—nine happy, busy, fruitful, and fulfilling years—and still no children—we again broached the subject of adoption. Imagine each other's surprise upon learning that we had *each thought* that the *other didn't* want to consider adoption. We could have thought, 'what a waste of time and years if only we had not misunderstood each other'. There really is no point in *'crying over spilt milk'*, as the proverb says.

Adoption in Africa is rare, an almost unheard-of concept. You see, since children are raised by a whole family, the children grow up knowing that they have a home, not only with their parents, but with any of their aunts and uncles or even grandparents. So, for us to pursue adoption was actually quite radical. We didn't know of anyone else who had legally adopted a totally unrelated child, but we felt it was good and right for us. So, we fulfilled all the requirements in terms of submitting medical, police, and social background reports and were registered as prospective adoptive parents with a Christian-run babies home that we had been introduced to.

One thing that occurred to us was that Kampala is not a large city, and we are quite well known, especially in Christian circles. We were concerned that it could be possible for a mother who had abandoned her baby to 'connect the dots', so to speak, and realise that a baby we had adopted could be hers. There is also little secrecy about the legal process of adoption here and that could also lead to a birth mother finding out where her previously abandoned baby had gone to. This procedure is not so much to stop the children from connecting with their birth family at the right time, but to stop any potential unwanted *begging*.

God answered that fear by giving us two beautiful babies, a boy and a girl, from a neighbouring country, so that any birth-family members would not be able to trace us. In fact, since both of our babies had been abandoned without trace of any birth family, short of a miracle, this can never arise. Someone told us that 'When the children arrive, your lives will never be the same again'. How very true that has proved! Our lives have been enriched by our lovely children. However we, as individuals, have had to learn a whole bunch of new skills as we care for these precious gifts that God has given us, with the responsibility of raising them for Him.

We brought them to Uganda under a guardianship order and to our surprise and delight, we were able to process the adoption in the High Court of Uganda. In many Western countries, it can take prospective adoptive parents years to be given a child, especially a baby. For us, it was a matter of four months, and that delay was caused by the legal paperwork required to obtain the guardianship order. When we brought John Mark and Abigail home, our niece, Brenda, was staying with us. She was one of those whose educational fees we had paid over a number of years. She had just graduated from university and was job hunting. Brenda loves children, so for the next six months, she cared for our two precious bundles of joy.

We were faced with the dilemma that all parents face: should I continue to work, or can we afford for a parent to stay at home and care for the children? I think that decision has to be made by each couple, as only they know their family circumstances. I continued to work, as I had Brenda's support as well as others in the family to help in caring for the babies. With time, we employed a nanny, and she looked after the growing children. I wished I could have remained at home, as I believe my role in the family as mother is to care for and nurture the children. There is no one who can care for your children like you can. However, it was not possible at the time, so we had to try to make the most of each moment with the children, trying to give quality of time where quantity was lacking.

We discovered that raising children is done differently in different parts of the world. Since we wanted to focus on a biblical approach to bringing up children, we decided on a two-fold strategy. Firstly, we would have other successful parents whom we asked to mentor us. By *successful*, we meant parents who have well-behaved children who love Jesus. And we also read any good books that could help us in setting the right framework within which we could raise John Mark and Abigail.

Just talking in a normal way to our babies is a foreign concept to most Ugandans. As a result, our children were very articulate even at age five and surprised many with their confidence and their vocabulary and sentence structure. We also insisted that anyone coming to visit the children, especially when they were babies, should first wash their hands, so as to avoid contamination with any germs on their hands. In this way, we largely avoided illness in the children. This was a strange custom to most of our visitors, but the history of the good health of the children has proved this to be a worthwhile practice. And I don't think we have lost any friends in the long run, either. Hopefully we might have encouraged other parents of babies to adopt the same custom.

Interestingly, after we made the decision to adopt, it seemed to open the gates for other couples we know to adopt! It's like we provoked them to think of adoption or gave them the courage to do 'the unusual' and adopt for themselves. How wonderful to think that we have given others the joy of parenthood! We now even have an association of adoptive parents in Kampala as a support group. Now, since the whole issue of legal adoption was hardly heard of in Africa, how did Chris's family react? How did Heather's family react to a couple of little brown children in the family?

We figured the reactions could be one of acceptance, indifference or rejection. That seems to be the standard response to anything considered to be *outside the norm* in whatever sphere of life—anything which is new or anything which challenges the status quo. Our marriage challenged the status quo in 1994, and we experienced all of those reactions then, but what about the arrival of our children? The majority of Chris's family were overjoyed at the news of our decision to adopt; the remaining one or two were won over when they met and got to know the children. Of course, the proof of the family's acceptance would probably be shown over such an issue as inheritance. Would the children be considered equals in the clan or family at that time? Our response to this possible scenario is to ensure we provide well enough for the children so that they never have to rely on family or clan support in the future.

My family were likewise thrilled for us and more so when we were able to take the children to the UK for a visit in September 2005, and they were able to meet them. My nephew's children are about the same age as ours, so they all had a whale of a time playing together. It is interesting that skin colour is never a barrier to children!

Chris has the responsibility of teaching the children his language. It was rather an uphill battle, since the language of our home is English, and the children attend an English-speaking school! I am also learning more of his language as he teaches

87

the children, so that is a good thing all round. Whilst the lack of a common language between Chris's mum and me means we never argue (!), it also means we find it difficult to establish a close relationship, as communication always has to be through an interpreter. So, this must be the means of better communication in the family on many levels.

CHAPTER 17

Encountering Corruption

Were there times when I felt like throwing in the towel and just leaving? Oh yes! Humanly speaking, I've been stretched to cope with things well outside of my comfort zone. Why am I still here (apart from the obvious reason of my husband, that is)? Firstly, I have to say it is because I am convinced this is where God wants me to be. Secondly, I do have a tenacious streak in me, and I hate to let anything get the better of me. Then lastly, I *have* to cope with any challenge now, since my home is here. I guess that boils down to one word—*commitment*.

I read somewhere that in life, obstacles will come, but it is whether we treat them as stumbling blocks or stepping stones that determines the outcome. I guess I've been stepping on a lot of stepping stones to get this far!

I had a run-in with the Uganda police force early on during my time here—not deliberately, I hasten to add. In fact, I'd been here only a matter of weeks when my boss asked me to go to a garage in the city to collect the MAF minibus that had been repaired. No problem, I thought. I knew the route, and he explained where the garage was. I collected the minibus and set off on the way back to the office.

Coming to a roundabout, I was in the process of turning left when a policeman standing on the kerb flagged me down. I stopped and waited while he looked around the vehicle. I was horrified and dismayed, and at first disbelieving when he told me I was driving the vehicle illegally! 'Your road licence has expired', he explained. When I also checked, I discovered he was right. None of us had realised it, and so I apologised, saying it was an oversight and that I was new in the country. I was, of course, hoping he would simply warn me and allow me to at least get back to the office. No way. He told me we would have to go to the central police station and go to court. And, I had to drive us both to the police station.

A million thoughts were going through my mind at this stage, and my heart was beating at least double the normal speed, at least that's what it felt like. I had been told the justice system in Uganda was not what it should be. Also, I had no money on me to pay a fine if, indeed, I did end up in court. Non-payment of a fine automatically means time in the notorious city jail. Mobile phones were not in use at that time, so I couldn't phone and let anyone know where I was or what was happening. What a predicament! I was almost feeling physically sick at this point.

I was taken to a room and told to wait while the officer filled out his report. I waited and waited. As I waited, I was silently crying to God for help. I asked the duty officer if I could use the telephone if I could pay for the call, but it wasn't allowed. Then I asked if I could go and make a call at the post office and was told I could if I left my ID card at the station. Great, I thought. At least I could go and arrange some sort of help.

On the way, I remembered I had no money (either for the fine that I thought was inevitable, or even to make a phone call), but I did have my cheque book. I had to head for the Foreign Exchange (or Forex) Bureau first to cash a cheque and get some money. Imagine my delight to see one of my colleagues, Sherry, in the Forex, getting money for herself! What an answer to prayer—I knew she would know what to do. Relief flooded over me as I shared with her what had happened. The owner of the Forex happened to overhear and intervened on my behalf. He told his staff member to go with me and 'take care of things'. Neither of us understood what he meant by that, but with hindsight, I suspect that a bribe was given, which was rather unfortunate. My ID card was returned, and the man was allowed to drive the vehicle out of the police yard, and he parked it at the kerb.

The challenge remained that the road licence had expired, so I had to go to a garage and hire garage plates to be able to legally drive the vehicle back to the office. Duly armed, I went to drive the van away from the police station. But, the van's accelerator wouldn't work. I couldn't believe it! The stupid van was just out of the garage, and now it had broken down, more-over right outside the very police station I had just been 'res-cued' from.

God was again at work. In the first office I went to, in a nearby building, there was a working phone line, and I was allowed to make the call to the MAF office. Sherry once again duly came to my rescue (all the other staff were busy, and she was the only one available). She had a look at the accelerator pedal and decided to drive to the garage to get a mechanic to look at it. Of course, by now it was lunchtime, so I had quite a wait. When he finally came and checked the accelerator for himself, he found it was fine. It seems that when Sherry had fiddled with the accelerator, she had replaced the clip that had come loose and so had fixed the problem herself! So, I had spent close to two hours sweating (literally and figuratively) outside the police station for nothing. As quickly as I could, I drove the minibus back to the office before anything else could happen.

I was exhausted mentally and emotionally after all this, but after a day or two, I could laugh at myself and my predica-ment. I guess the experience was a major stepping stone - if it had been a real stone, I would gladly have thrown it at that minibus! Well, maybe not literally, but I did refuse to drive that vehicle ever again. I was glad to see the back of it; in fact, I cheered when it was finally sold.

Car stories abound since they are the easiest and most comfortable way of getting around; you tend to drive every-where you go. For me, being able to drive was incredibly freeing. I didn't have to depend on anyone else to go anywhere, and I had the use of a small MAF car for business and personal use. A couple of weeks later, I went into the city to do a few errands. In those days, we bought fresh farm milk, which we then had to boil in case of brucellosis or any other milk-borne disease. We used a large five-litre insulated container to buy enough for every MAF family, and then we shared it out accordingly. It was my turn to buy this day, as I was going to the same area to take care of other MAF business.

Having finished the other business, I bought the milk and was heading out of the building and back to the car when I had to stop because of the rain. Now, I need to explain. Coming from Britain, we know all about the rain. It is cold and wet, but you get bundled up and get on with life; the rain doesn't stop you from doing what you need to do, right? Now, as I looked out at the rain, I forgot that this was Uganda with torrential equatorial rain. Mistake number one: African rain drops are huge and get you soaked through in *seconds*. I was thinking, I'll just use the umbrella and get to the car, which was just across the street. Mistake number two: I didn't stop to ask myself why about thirty other people had the wisdom to take shelter and wait for the rain to pass over.

So, I got the car keys out of my bag and held them in my hand, ready to open the car door. Umbrella in one hand, large heavy handbag over the other shoulder, heavy milk container with five litres of milk in it over the arm and car keys in hand. Out I stepped as, fortunately for me, the rain was beginning to ease a little. I hadn't bargained for the raging stream I had to cross. With the volume of rain, the gutter at the side of the road had become a fast-flowing torrent, which was no problem with my long legs, I thought as I stepped out. I still would have managed if my Scholl sandal hadn't come off my foot—and remained at the other side of the rushing water.

As I bent down and stretched back to pick it up, the heavy handbag slipped off my shoulder and knocked the car keys out of my hand and into the raging water. They disappeared instantly. Shock and horror! How could that happen? Oh no! At least I recovered the shoe, though I got rather wet in the process, and I had no choice but to retreat back to the shelter of the building to think what to do next. The crowd of wise, sensible *dry* people must have had a lot of laughs at this impatient white woman who didn't have the sense to wait even a mere ten minutes till the rain stopped, which of course it did— African rain is very heavy but usually lasts only a short time before the sun comes out again.

I hadn't used the public transport system at all yet, so I decided to walk to the nearby theatre car park where I would be able to hire a taxi to take me back to the office. God was again allowing me to be stretched, but not over-stretched. As I got to the top of the street, my colleague's husband just happened to be driving past. So, I got a lift right back to the MAF office. My Ugandan colleagues had quite a few laughs at my expense, and I learned a few lessons myself.

Later that day, as we didn't have a spare key for the car, we had to get a tow truck to take the car to the garage where they could replace the door locks and steering column lock. I watched while the tow truck gang put the hook under the front of the car and lifted it off the ground. They then went to the back of the car and all of them put their hands under the back of the car and started lifting and bouncing it up and down in rhythm. As they bounced and lifted, they were gradually bouncing the back of the car away from the kerb. I was very keen to ask why but decided to keep quiet and watch.

The young men then all jumped into the cab of the tow truck and obviously let off the handbrake, as the tow truck - with my car lifted up behind it - started to roll backwards downhill. I was speechless at this, and before I could find any words to say, the driver put the tow truck into gear and the engine roared to life. He then braked hard to stop the downhill motion and the two vehicles jerked to a halt, with my car rolling back and forth on the towing hook. They actually jump-started the tow truck, backwards, downhill, with my car in tow!

This could happen only in Africa, I thought in amazement. The driver must have been a good driver to have accomplished that feat, though I didn't think about that at the time.

Over the years, the number of vehicles on the roads has increased enormously. And yet the roads' infrastructure remains more or less the same. The result is traffic jams, drivers getting their permits by bribing the officials instead of sitting for their driving test, and hardly anyone following the highway code. I have come to the conclusion that there are only two rules governing driving on Uganda's roads: firstly, the bigger you are, the more right of way you have. Secondly, if you see a space, head for it. That means if you are in a traffic jam, and you can see a space in front of you, then you have to take that space before someone else does. The fact that you completely block the junction and the flow of traffic in all directions is immaterial. This either drives you nuts, or you learn to be patient. Through of all this, I have most certainly grown. However, the incidents that drove me to the end of my tether were two cases of theft. It was the proverbial straw that almost broke the camel's back.

It is the background to the thefts that made the incident of greater significance than it really warranted. In November 1997, I had driven home in the MAF vehicle allocated to me and had stopped at the gate to our home, waiting for someone to open up and let me in. A man seemed to appear from nowhere, opened the car door and told me to get out of the car. For once, I did as I was told and only after getting out and having my handbag wrenched out of my grip, did I see another man with a sawn-off shotgun in his hand, which was covered by the anorak he was wearing. The two men, with a third accomplice whom I hadn't noticed, jumped into the car, reversed quickly and sped off in a cloud of dust. Only then did it dawn on me that they had actually stolen the vehicle!

To cut a long story short, the vehicle, my handbag and my briefcase were all recovered within twenty-four hours, due to an amazing series of coincidences that I would call miraculous answers to prayer. However, it took me quite a few weeks to get over the fear that seemed to follow me whenever I drove in a car. I was just getting back on an even keel, though still somewhat stressed, when Chris was driving me to church one day. At an intersection in the middle of the city, a pickup banged into the back wing of the car. Chris got out, checking what damage had been caused, and I got out, too. I left the car door open and stood listening. All of a sudden, I saw a guy, who was clutching something, run away up the road on the opposite side of the junction. A policeman saw him and gave chase, whereupon he threw away the bag he had been holding into the middle of the road.

The bystanders who had gathered to watch the proceedings were shouting in our direction, and I thought it had to do with the car accident. In fact, they were calling to me—it was *my* bag that the thief had taken from our car behind my back, and now it was lying thrown away in the middle of the road!

I ran over and picked it up—contents intact—and so many emotions were washing over me at this point. I was close to tears. I was angry at myself for leaving the car door open, I was furious that someone could take advantage of our car accident to try to rob me as well. I was embarrassed at my stupidity in not realising what was going on, that it was my bag lying in the road. Not to mention, I was mad at the negligent driver who had caused the accident in the first place.

I sat back in the car, with tears welling in my eyes, and yelled, *'What on earth am I doing in this God-forsaken place?'* It was a real cry of anguish from the depth of my heart. But if I had been offered an air ticket to the UK at that point, I don't think I would have accepted it, though I would have been very tempted! However, I did scare Chris and had to spend time reassuring him after I had calmed down.

I was at the end of my own strength through this series of incidents, but that's when God took over and gave me His strength to keep going and not stumble but rise above the challenge.

CHAPTER 18

Cross-Cultural Paradigms

One important thing that has helped me, over time, to successfully adapt to life in Uganda, was being able to undergo a paradigm shift in my worldview or my thinking over a number of issues. What do I mean by this? When you move from a place where you know how everything works, where you know the values and behavioural systems that society operates by and where you are used to the *normal* way of doing things, and then you move to a place where none of these apply, you have to go through a change in thinking that redefines what is *normal*, what you are used to.

In 1991, the only 'supermarket' in Kampala was no bigger (and less well-stocked) than the average village shop. It was the only place to buy breakfast cereals, but they were so expensive that I didn't bother. The cheapest place to buy basic groceries was at the central Nakasero Market. There were small shops surrounding the main fruit-and-vegetable market, each selling the same limited range of basic staples. Of course, you didn't pay the first price that the shop owner asked for; you had to bargain over *everything*. It sure added to the shopping time.

Being a butcher's daughter, I was used to pristine, refrigerated counters, laid out with every possible cut of beef, pork, lamb and so on. The reality in Kampala was quite different. The meat section of Nakasero Market consisted of around ten outdoor stalls, each having a side of beef (or what I thought was lamb, but which I soon discovered was goat) hanging up.

The butcher, or rather meat-seller, had no clue about different cuts of meat. To him meat was meat and all you decide is how much you want to buy. He would then hack off a lump—bone, fat, and all—-and toss it on the grubby fly-infested scales. The meat was always tough and required several hours' cooking to make it tender. The good side to this (oh yes, there is one) is that practically all the meat in Uganda is free of the growth hormones that are usually used on cattle reared in the West. The cows are also grazed on grass and pasture which has not been fertilised, and so the meat and vegetables that are sold are largely organic. That has to be healthier!

I had to buy a new handbag shortly after my arrival to carry the large volumes of bank notes that I would get whenever I would cash a personal cheque at the Forex Bureau. At that time, the largest denomination note available was for two hundred Uganda shillings, so when I would cash a cheque for £100, I would receive 120,000 shillings. If I was lucky enough to get 200 shilling notes, that meant a total of 600 actual notes, tied in bundles of 100 each! However, if all I could get were 100 shilling notes, (or worse still, 50 shilling notes) that meant 1,200 notes or more. So, I had a large shoulder bag to accommodate the currency, never mind personal items. It was also rather heavy and almost wore a groove across my shoulder. It would have made a good weapon against a bag snatcher, not that I ever needed it for that. One swipe with a bag full of notes, and the thief would be unconscious!

Something else I had to learn to take seriously were snakes. In Britain, there is only one poisonous snake, the adder, and it is rare and its bite rarely fatal. In Africa, there are many poisonous species, a bite from which can cause death within minutes. I knew these facts but had no idea what to do when actually confronted with a snake one morning, wriggling from my sitting room towards the kitchen. Admittedly, it wasn't a big one, maybe only twelve to fifteen inches long, but it was long enough for me! I froze, got instantaneous goose bumps and did the only thing I could think of—-I threw the umbrella

I was carrying at it! Of course, it didn't hurt the snake and it just slithered into the kitchen and disappeared in between two cupboards. What a relief! It took quite a few minutes though before the goose bumps disappeared and my heart stopped thumping in my chest.

Since I had been on my way out to the office, I picked up the umbrella and my bag and sidled carefully and watchfully through the kitchen to the back door. Thank goodness, I couldn't see the snake. I had relaxed by the time I got to the office and just by way of casual conversation, mentioned it to Ruth, the office receptionist. *'A snake in your house?'* she screamed. *'What did you do? Did you kill it?'*

'Well, er, actually, no. It disappeared behind the kitchen cupboard', I replied, a bit taken aback by her agitated response.

'You can't leave it there; we have to find it and kill it', she announced. I could see she was shocked by my apparent lack of concern and thought I was daft, leaving such a dangerous creature on the loose in my house. So, we walked back over to my house, accompanied by two MAF customers who were also concerned for my safety, and looked for the offending snake! I guess there must have been a way out behind the kitchen cupboard, as we never did find it. I kept a watchful eye in the sitting room and kitchen for a few days and then forgot about it. Ruth didn't, though, and kept asking me for several weeks whether I had found it and killed it yet.

My second snake encounter happened on my second visit to the village. I had gone to bathe in the grass-walled outdoor 'bathroom' and was standing in my birthday suit, ready to begin splashing water on myself. However, out of the corner of my eye I saw the snake slithering into the grass wall, just in front of where I was standing. I hesitated, wondering whether to continue bathing or get dressed again and go and tell Chris about the encounter. Then I remembered Ruth's reaction to the snake in my home and decided I'd better go and tell Chris.

'A snake in the bathing place'! he exclaimed. He immediately shouted in Luo to the boys around the home, and we

all ran to the bathing place, so I could show them where the snake had gone. Sure enough, it was still there, and the boys, armed with long sticks, did not rest until the thing was well and truly beaten to death. From all of this, I have learned to give snakes a very wide berth. Fortunately for me, the snakes are not too keen on me either, and I thankfully have seen very few in my time here. At least I know what I am supposed to do now, should I ever have another close encounter.

One thing that *does* give me serious goose-bumps is grass-hoppers. I have to admit that these creatures are harmless (at least to humans); however, the very *sight* of them makes my flesh crawl, and I want to run away. They come in seasons and one particular office that I occupied in the church building seemed to be a collecting point for grasshoppers! How they got in, I never found out, but in the mornings, there would be up to ten of these creatures *inside the office itself* or just out-side in the foyer! I used to call for a caretaker or security guard to come and catch them and remove them. Imagine thinking they had all been removed only to discover as you sit down that there is one crawling on the underside of the desk—arrgh! As for me picking one up to throw it out of the window—no way, thank you! I really have to steel myself to walk past one in case it takes off and starts flying around.

One time when we were driving to Kenya, we stopped at a hotel in Kericho for lunch. The children were with us, and I took Abby to the toilet. Imagine my horror on entering the washroom as I could see grasshoppers crawling on the walls and even the ceiling! Now I don't want Abby growing up with this irrational fear that I have, so I had to ignore the cold sweat I had broken out with and get on with what we had to do. It got worse, however, when we entered the toilet stall. There was a grasshopper on the wall behind the cistern, but as I turned round to lock the door, I came *literally* face to face with one on the back of the door. I swallowed hard, tried to keep my voice at its usual pitch and concentrate on Abby, praying in my heart that these things would not start flying around! Fortunately, during daytime, the grasshoppers are more sluggish then and are not as active as they are at night when they fly around, trying to get to a light source. However I was *so* glad just to get out of there.

All of this is hilarious to Ugandans, as they love to catch the grasshoppers to cook and make into a traditional delicacy. Yes, they are indeed edible, though I have been unable to bring myself to try one as yet. While we are on the subject of preparing food, I remember the first meal I prepared for Chris. He had come to my house with his cousin, William, and I left them talking in the living room as I finished the cooking. As I had learned many years ago from my mother, I placed the plates in the oven to warm up. I put the tureens of food and the now-hot plates on the table. As we sat down, I warned the guys that the plates were hot so that they would not burn their fingers.

'Why have you warmed the plates?' asked Chris.

'To keep the food hot', I answered, while thinking that the answer was rather obvious.

Meanwhile, Chris asked, 'Why on earth would you want to keep the food hot when the weather is so hot anyway?' Um, good question.

Where I grew up, we always heated the plates that the food would be served on in order to keep the food hot in the cold weather particularly. My mother's admonition, 'Eat up—the food's no good to you cold', was ringing in my ears as Chris's logical question challenged this almost hallowed meal-time principle. I had to agree that the plate warming no longer had the significance and importance in Uganda that it had in the UK. I no longer warm plates.

Something I realised quite early on in my time here is that Ugandans are not shy when it comes to expressing their love for God. There is no embarrassment in worship or in praying out loud—in fact prayer time in most churches is when all the congregation will pray out loud all at the same time! Some may talk quietly, but many will be very passionate, and some may even weep as they commune with their heavenly Father. For a Brit, where we regard such things as private, it took me some time to get used to it and to be able to 'switch off' the voices around about me and concentrate on praying and worshipping myself.

When I started dating Chris, on the other hand, he refused to hold my hand in public. The reason was that people would automatically assume we were sleeping together if we were seen holding hands. Even in the privacy of our own home after we were married, it was very difficult for him to openly show any affection, especially when there were other people in the house. What a contrast! Ugandans are very demonstrative in their love for God and very secretive in showing love for one another. Western culture on the other hand is secretive about anything pertaining to God and is blatantly sensual and sex-saturated in just about every other aspect of life.

You might deduce from this that sex was, and to some extent still is, a taboo subject in most cultures in Uganda. For those brought up in rural areas, the marriage preparation customs are quite different. The bride to be would be taken off usually by her mother's sister for a few days prior to her wedding to be taught how to please a man. This would include how to run a household, the cultural expectations he would have of her kneeling to greet him to show respect, and yes, how to please him sexually. The woman is not supposed to enjoy herself in the marriage bed but should simply satisfy her husband and bear him children. Sex is supposed to take place under the bed covers and in the dark.

Now, many of these customs are dying out, due to the influx of Western culture largely though the media, but these attitudes may still be present in the back of a person's mind and could form unconscious expectations of a future spouse's behaviour. This is another reason why I believe that the more time an intending couple invests in counselling before the marriage, the greater chance that marriage has of success.

Chris adopted three interesting rules of behaviour that governed his conduct as a single man: 'never alone; never in the dark; and never horizontal'. In other words, if he was with a girl, he would never be in a private place totally alone with her, never with her in a dark place and never in a horizontal position. I thought that was a wise code of conduct for anyone wishing to honour God by remaining sexually pure. However, I am sure this would be considered puritanical to anyone reading this from a Western culture, where sexual purity is often not stressed as a virtue anymore (even though it is required of anyone wishing to please God, according to Jesus).

CHAPTER 19

Cross-Cultural Compliments

S o, what makes a successful relationship, especially one of two different cultures? We are, by no means, the experts but offer the following as something that has worked for us and for other couples that we have known and observed for a number of years. First of all, who wears the trousers in your relationship? Much of the thinking these days is that a man and a woman are totally equal in marriage—in rights, in decisions, in household tasks, in everything, in fact. Therefore, the man *must* help around the house, and the woman can take *responsibility* for decisions in the family. In other words, both can be the boss of the house. Unfortunately, that can lead to disputes and arguments when the couple are not in agreement.

What is the answer to that dilemma? I believe the Bible has the right model for a well-functioning family. It clearly states that before God, a man and a woman are equal in value. However, within marriage, the man and the woman are given different roles and responsibilities. Thus, the husband is the protector, the provider, and the one given *ultimate* responsibility for the decisions in the family. A wise and caring husband will, of course, consult his wife and best friend over the major decisions that they face, but ultimately, he is responsible for the outcome. Now that I understand my husband's role in our family, I'm not sure I would like to have the weight of that responsibility! It sure makes me pray for him all the more and encourage him whenever I can.

Whilst some wives and mothers choose to work, their role and responsibility is also that of homemaker and mother—that's how women are naturally gifted. I have worked most of my adult life, but when children came into our family, I began to understand the homemaking role much more, and value it as a truly honourable and fulfilling one. So, what is the answer for the wife if she finds herself torn between working and looking after the home and the children? In Uganda, many wives work and even study in addition to their role in the home. Since labour is so cheap here, it is easy to employ someone to do the housework and cooking and a nanny to look after the children. Often, they are one and the same person. Then at least she can contribute towards the family income and enjoy her career.

I am not going to give a 'right' answer to this dilemma; I will merely outline the process I went through when children arrived. At that time, we had a house loan to pay off, and it would have been extremely difficult to manage on one salary only. So, we prayed for the right nanny to employ so that I could continue working. We had one for some time and then had to relieve her of her duties, as she was not good at disciplining two lively three-year-olds. Fortunately, we had another niece who was available at the time to help out until we could find a new nanny.

However, during that time, I realised that I would actually prefer to be at home raising my children, not employing someone else who, after all, would still not raise my children quite the same way I would. Besides that, since they are my children, the responsibility for raising them in a God-fearing way is also mine, together with my husband. I guess working from home would provide the best option, but such opportunities are few and far between.

In our pre-marriage counselling, we had five sessions of at least one hour each on different aspects of marriage. The last session, for some reason, was cancelled and we never got around to fitting it in. The subject was resolving conflict, and with hindsight, we might have saved ourselves some trouble if we had managed to fit it in! However, there is no teacher quite like personal experience, so maybe the way we had to learn our lessons on this subject were well learned through the experience itself.

To me, the first way to resolve conflict is not to take offence unnecessarily. Some things are just not worth fighting or arguing over. Ask God for His grace and patience, instead, to work in you. A good example of this is when one partner is very tidy, and the other is the opposite. If the untidy partner cannot change out of love and respect for you, after you have calmly discussed the matter, then the tidy person either has to do the tidying up, or he or she must learn to live with the untidiness of their partner. Untidiness is not a dangerous or life-threatening issue, so it may be better to put up with it, rather than create an unpleasant home environment over it.

Another way to avoid unnecessary conflict is to make sure you have really understood what your spouse meant—rather than what you thought you heard. Quite often, our listening skills are not as sharp as they need to be, or we misunderstand our spouse's intention in their words. A good thing to do before blowing your top is to ask, 'You said *so and so*, but what did you actually mean?' or 'I heard you say .... Is that what you actually meant?' This really happened between Chris and me while we were dating, and it was a good thing I asked him, as what I thought he had said and what in fact *he did say* were two completely different things. This is all the more true in a cross-cultural situation where at least one partner may not be speaking their mother tongue.

Another thing that made a great difference to the way I looked at disagreements was when Chris told me, 'You know I love you so much that I would never deliberately set out to hurt you. Yes, I may tread on your toes, I may say things I should not say, but I would never deliberately hurt you'. That changed my attitude towards our arguments and, in fact, made me much less likely to take offence. Instead, I would try more to see his point of view and understand where he was coming from.

A great truth I learned early in my days in Uganda was when a Ugandan office staff member told me, 'You can choose not to get angry'. That made me think, as I had not realised that anger, indeed my response to any situation, is a choice I make. These two revelations and the power of God working in my life have certainly helped me to become a much-less-reactive person.

I am the type who can flare up easily, say my piece, and then calm down again very quickly. Chris, on the other hand, takes time to boil over, but when he does, it is like a volcano! He had to learn to deal with irritations as they happened and not wait until he had a list of four or five of my 'misdemeanours' before the pressure got too much and he blew up! He has a very good memory and can remember conversations almost verbatim. So, he also had to learn not to keep a list of wrongs (as Paul's letter to the Corinthians points out) to remind me about when I'd failed him, yet again.

There are two biblical proverbs that say, 'A word aptly spoken is like apples of gold in settings of silver', and 'A gentle answer turns away wrath'. I have proven that a gentle answer is the best response in any heated situation. It certainly does not fuel the argument, and it is much easier to *apologise* and *make up*, when fewer unnecessary and hurtful words have been exchanged. The right word at the right time is always a blessing and can, indeed, diffuse tension before it becomes too great.

One necessary phrase in any argument that is both gentle and appropriate is a sincere 'I am sorry'. Both parties need to be humble and contrite enough to apologise when they are in the wrong. And the greater leader is the one who takes the initiative and apologises for the hurt they have caused, even when they feel they didn't start the fight.

Chris and I have endeavoured not to let any walls grow up between us, or another way of putting it is, to not to let any distance come between us. We do as much as possible together; for example, I had to get interested in football, and he has had to put up with accompanying me for grocery shopping once in a while! I believe that is another reason why God made it possible for me to join staff at church a number of years ago so that we could share as many common interests and enjoy as much time together as possible.

There have been times when we have been too busy to devote enough time and attention to each other. We can gradually drift into our own worlds and further apart. This is almost inevitable in today's busy lifestyles; however, when you realise it has happened, you take remedial action straightaway! We sit and talk, and set goals about how much time we must spend together, going home from work *on time* in order to reconnect with each other. It takes time and effort, but the reward is a truly fulfilling marriage.

One vitally important factor in keeping us together and actively working at our relationship is the fact that we regard our marriage as a *covenant* relationship. What do I mean? Is that the same as a contract? No, it is not. A contract can be broken at any time either party considers the terms of the contract have been breached. A covenant, on the other hand, is an unbreakable promise, made before God. We are in the relationship for keeps—there is no way out, since divorce in not an option, we are in it 'till death do us part'. So, sorting out our differences becomes an essential part of our lives. It certainly makes you mature quickly, as an immature person is not someone pleasant to live with! Since we purpose to deal with issues as they arise, it means we can get on with enjoying our marriage the rest of the time. We are not wasting emotional energy on fuming with each other or being bitter or resentful. What a recipe for a happy healthy home!

CONCLUSION

There are eternal biblical principles that go beyond any cross-cultural divide, which if applied in any marriage, would make that marriage thrive in spite of cultural or other differences one may encounter. When we applied these simple biblical principles in our relationship and marriage, instead of just surviving, our marriage has thrived against all odds of cross-cultural differences. As time has gone on, we do, in fact, have fewer conflicts, and we are better at resolving them when they do arise. Our marriage just keeps on getting better by the grace of God and the help of His Holy Spirit.

The common faith that we have in Jesus Christ, this kind of irrevocable commitment to one another, our love for each other and the friendship we share draws us closer to God and closer to each other. We face the challenges of life together, prayerfully, and in agreement with one another. We have resolved that no one and nothing will come between us, not even our beautiful, beloved children. This kind of stable home environment gives the children such a sense of security and a safe place where they can explore and grow into fulfilling all the potential that God has placed in them.

So how do you keep your marriage from becoming just *routine*? How can you keep it fresh? How do you stay in love with the same person year in and year out? Here are a few thoughts:

- Keep on doing the romantic things you used to do while you were getting to know each other, and continually be thinking of how to add new, special ones.

111

- Do things that you know will please your spouse.
- Don't do things that you know your spouse does not like.
- Share everything together, from your daily experiences, your interests, to your hopes, dreams and fears.
- Remind each other *constantly* that you love each other.
- Wife, be your husband's number one fan and keep yourself looking good for him.
- Husband, be a listening ear to your wife, and encourage her to grow into the woman God intended her to be.
- Plan to have fun time together and go out on dates regularly—as often as you can.
- Your life must be an open book to your spouse in terms of finance, sex, plans, fears or any other concerns—however trivial the issue may appear.
- We keep no secret between us.
- We keep no records of wrongs.
- We focus on the positives.

Why not ask each other what each of you would like the other to do to keep your love alive and kicking? You might get some interesting answers, but why not have fun together and invest in your relationship at the same time?

Of course, we never know what the future holds, but we know Who holds our future. Chris and I would not change our lives for anything else, or anyone else on this planet earth.

As I close, I trust and pray that this story will have been of some use to you and will have given you a laugh or a smile of empathy as you have caught a glimpse into another world, *our world*.

God bless you.

AFTERWORD

A number of years have passed since the events described in this book, though the memories are a fresh as yesterday and bring the same smiles to our lips as when we first experienced them—or in a few cases, a while later!

Those were definitely years of God graciously working in and through our lives, refining us to be better vessels for use in His service (see 2 Timothy 2:20–21), and making us fit together as husband and wife. A good analogy of such a partnership is a socket and a plug, fitting together closely and snugly.

When I prayerfully looked back over the last twenty-five years or so, I felt God prompting me to look at John, chapter 15. Jesus told us *He is the true vine, and we as His children are branches of that same vine.* We can't exist if we are *not* connected to the vine, but if we *are* connected to the vine, He promises us that we will bear fruit: 'Remain in me, as I also remain in you. No branch can bear fruit by itself; it must remain in the vine. Neither can you bear fruit unless you remain in me' (v. 4).

However, alongside the promise to bear fruit is also the promise of pruning—not such an attractive prospect. Verse 2 says: 'He cuts off every branch in me that bears no fruit, while every branch that does bear fruit he prunes so that it will be even more fruitful'. Pruning sounds, and is, painful, but it is very productive as it results in the branch being 'even more fruitful'. The experiences we have related in this book represent the process of a branch growing, bearing some fruit, being pruned, and then bearing more fruit.

113

Even as God was grooming us to bear more fruit in the years leading up to 2005, the Lord was preparing us for even greater things and great service in His Kingdom. Verse 8 says: 'This is to my Father's glory, that you bear *much* fruit, showing yourselves to be my disciples'.

Why should God choose us for this awesome task and responsibility? I really haven't the faintest idea, as we are nothing of, and in, ourselves. What and who we are is simply the work of God's grace in and through us. Chris says possibly because we are FAST—Faithful, Available, Servant-hearted, and Teachable!

But the next stage of our personal and spiritual growth— the bearing of *much* fruit—has to wait for the next book.

CPSIA information can be obtained
at www.ICGtesting.com
Printed in the USA
FFHW021846261218
49969121-54706FF